Woodrow Wilson

A LIPPER/VIKING BOOK

Larry McMurtry on Crazy Horse
Edmund White on Marcel Proust
Peter Gay on Mozart
Garry Wills on Saint Augustine
Jonathan Spence on Mao Zedong
Edna O'Brien on James Joyce
Jane Smiley on Charles Dickens
Carol Shields on Jane Austen
Mary Gordon on Joan of Arc
Karen Armstrong on the Buddha
Patricia Bosworth on Marlon Brando
R. W. B. Lewis on Dante
Janet Malcolm on Anton Chekhov
Marshall Frady on Martin Luther King, Jr.
Elizabeth Hardwick on Herman Melville
John Keegan on Winston Churchill
Wayne Koestenbaum on Andy Warhol
Roy Blount, Jr., on Robert E. Lee
David Quammen on Charles Darwin
Sherwin Nuland on Leonardo da Vinci
Nigel Nicolson on Virginia Woolf
Bobbie Ann Mason on Elvis Presley
Douglas Brinkley on Rosa Parks
Francine du Plessix Gray on Simone Weil
Thomas Cahill on Pope John XXIII

LOUIS AUCHINCLOSS

Woodrow Wilson

A Penguin Life

A LIPPER/VIKING BOOK

VIKING
Published by the Penguin Group
Penguin Putnam Inc., 375 Hudson Street,
New York, New York 10014, U.S.A.
Penguin Books Ltd, 27 Wrights Lane, London W8 5TZ, England
Penguin Books Australia Ltd, Ringwood, Victoria, Australia
Penguin Books Canada Ltd, 10 Alcorn Avenue,
Toronto, Ontario, Canada M4V 3B2
Penguin Books (N.Z.) Ltd, 182–190 Wairau Road,
Auckland 10, New Zealand

Penguin Books Ltd, Registered Offices:
Harmondsworth, Middlesex, England

First published in 2000 by Viking Penguin,
a member of Penguin Putnam Inc.

3   5   7   9   10   8   6   4   2

Grateful acknowledgment is made for permission to reprint excerpts from
Intimate Papers of Colonel House, edited by Charles Seymour. Copyright ©
1928, 1956 by Charles Seymour. Reprinted by permission of Houghton Mifflin
Company. All rights reserved.

LIBRARY OF CONGRESS CATALOGING-IN-PUBLICATION DATA
Auchincloss, Louis.
Woodrow Wilson / Louis Auchincloss.
p.   cm.—(Penguin lives series)
"A Lipper/Viking book."
Includes bibliographical references.
ISBN 0-670-88904-0
1. Wilson, Woodrow, 1856–1924.   2. Presidents—United States—
Biography.   I. Title.   II. Series.
E767.A88 2000
973.91'3'092—dc21   99–046890

This book is printed on acid-free paper.

∞

Printed in the United States of America
Set in Berling
Designed by Francesca Belanger

For Arthur Schlesinger, Jr.

Woodrow Wilson

1

AT THE END OF SEPTEMBER, in 1919, the presidential train bearing Woodrow Wilson on a western tour of speech-making in his last-ditch, desperate effort to rally the nation behind the ratification of the Versailles Treaty of Peace, which the Senate seemed determined to nullify, pulled into Wichita, Kansas, where a large crowd had gathered at the station to hear him. After a fifteen-minute wait the president's secretary, Joe Tumulty, appeared and announced gravely that his chief was suffering from "nervous exhaustion" and could not make the address. The train then headed directly to Washington.

Wilson had suffered a transient ischemic attack, the prelude to a major stroke, an occlusion of the right middle cerebral artery, which occurred at the White House on October 2, felling him to the floor of his bathroom, paralyzing his left side and rendering him essentially incompetent. Edith Bolling Wilson, his wife, and Admiral Cary Grayson, his devoted doctor, moved quickly to close the doors and hide his condition from all, but Ike Hoover of the White House staff made this entry in his diary: "The President lay stretched out on the large Lincoln bed. He looked as if dead. There was not a sign of life. His face bore a long cut above the temple from which the signs of blood were still evident. . . . He was just gone as far as anyone could judge from appearances."

There followed a strange hiatus in American governance. As biographer August Heckscher has put it: "During this period no proclamations were issued, no pardons granted, bills became laws without a signature. The regular meetings of cabinet members gave the country the impression that some matters were being dealt with. They sat, these lieutenants who had once gathered around a formidable chief, discussing for the most part trivial matters, and even then were often unable to make decisions."

Edith Wilson would sometimes meet with the cabinet and take papers with questions to the president, always behind closed doors, returning with a "He says yes" or a "He says no." Had she read them to him? Or had she made up the answers? Nobody knew.

Her later defense in keeping all news from the public and barring all but family visitors from the sickbed was that any anxiety might have been fatal to her husband, and her ultimate justification, she would claim, was that he *did* get better and was eventually able to function more or less like his old self. But it was mostly less. Her excuse that she had no interest in the president of the United States but only in her husband was less that of a free American woman than of a Hindu wife who has no obligation to society beyond that of her duty to her lord and master, ending with that of throwing herself on his funeral pyre. Even had there been any validity in her exaggerated fear that any frank revelation of his health might have been fatal to her husband, was the proper governance of her nation not as much worth his dying for as the victory abroad for which he had asked thousands of young men to give their lives? For Grayson, anyway, as a doctor and naval officer, there seems no excuse.

The Wilson who at last recovered some of his health was a pale simulacrum of the man he had been. He was querulous, petulant, and unable to take care of business with anything like the wonderful efficiency that had characterized his former activities. And anticipating the Democratic Convention of 1920 in San Francisco, though he walked with difficulty, supported by an aide and dragging his left leg, and though he could not arise from a chair without assistance, and even though he had once told Grayson that the country was suffering ill effects from his sickness and he should resign his office, he now embarrassed his intimates by insisting that he would seek a third term! Even the loyal Grayson now had to brief Senator Carter Glass on the impossibility of this.

His stroke, however, had not been his first. He had suffered one in Princeton in his academic days and another in Paris during the peace talks, and though in each case his recovery had seemed complete, there is evidence that these strokes took some toll on his temperament. We shall see that there were always two Woodrow Wilsons, and that the tragedy of his bad health understandably contributed to the lesser and not the greater of the two. This ambivalence in a man so admired confused many who observed him closely. I believe it confused himself.

3

*   *   *

The twenty-eighth president of the United States was born a southerner, but his family had just arrived in the South. His father, Joseph Ruggles Wilson, an Ohio printer turned Presbyterian preacher, was the son of a Scotch-Irish immigrant, and his mother, Jessie Woodrow, had been born in England, daughter of a minister of the same denomination.

Joseph Wilson left Ohio when he accepted a call from the First Presbyterian Church of Staunton, Virginia, in which town his eldest son, Thomas Woodrow, was born in 1856. Two years later the now Doctor of Divinity Wilson moved his family to Augusta, Georgia, where he occupied one of the most important pulpits in the South, rising to be the chief executive of the Southern Presbyterian Church. On both sides of his family, therefore, the future president inherited a faith in a God who premised the forgiveness of original sin on man's unquestioning worship and offered eternal life for his obedience to divine law.

It was to be the major force of his life. He has frequently been compared to Gladstone as a statesman permeated with a sense of religion. It must have seemed to him that God had destined Woodrow Wilson to dedicate himself to providing good governance, directly or indirectly, to a nation that many, perhaps even most, Americans believed to have been endowed by the deity with a glorious future to be an example to the world. And Wilson, in seeking to emulate his God, in aiming perhaps to fulfill his destiny as a kind of minor prophet, would ultimately take on some of the characteristics of a supreme judge, even those demonstrated in the Old Testament, of wrath as well as benevolence. For if he could be harsh and authoritarian in his moral judgments, he could also be humble and kind. The president who could threaten to "crush" his opponents in Congress could also be the affectionate father and husband who loved to read Wordsworth and Browning aloud to his family and indulge in skits and charades.

Joseph Wilson, a brilliant and popular preacher and a man of an outgoing and cheerful disposition, did not find slavery inconsistent with his faith, and he sided enthusiastically with the Confederacy. His son grew up to view sympathetically the stricken and occupied South; as a little boy he had seen Robert E. Lee pass through Atlanta after the surrender, and standing by his father and looking up into the general's face, he had, as August Heckscher has put it, "perhaps his first intimation of what defeat meant and how it could be borne."

Wilson's claim to be a southerner had in it something of the factitious. Although it is true that he lived in Virginia and Georgia until he was in his late twenties, he had no southern ancestry, and he resided in the North for the balance of his life. There is more than a touch of sentimentality in his nostalgic attraction to the elegance and gracious living of the antebellum planters and their gallant fighting for a lost cause. He used to say that the South was the only part of the country where nothing had to be explained to him. As Henry Wilkinson Bragdon put it: "He was a Southerner in his courtly manners, in his attitude towards women, and in the hospitality with which he received

5

numberless in-laws and cousins into his home. He was curiously indifferent to the moral iniquity of slavery and accepted uncritically the post-Reconstruction arrangements to keep the Negro in his place."

But it stopped there. Nobody was a greater supporter of the federal union. Even as a youth he deemed a Decoration Day for the Union dead a means of sustaining national bitterness, and only fifteen years after Appomattox, as a University of Virginia student, he approved in a speech the restoration of the union. The old South he relegated to history and romance; the political Wilson was a man of his time. He ultimately came to view the loss of the war as an actual benefit to the South, ridding it as it did of slavery and keeping it in God's union, though he never quite shook off the condescending southern attitude toward blacks, and his first administration was stained by his allowing segregation in certain government buildings. He did this, it has been said, only to enlist the support of southern members of his cabinet and congressman for his social legislation, but as late as 1915 we find him writing to his second wife, whose niece wished to marry a Panamanian: "It would be bad enough at best to have anyone we love marry into a Central American family, because there is the presumption that the blood is not unmixed." Still, nine out of ten men raised as he was would have thought the same.

The young Woodrow, or Tommy as he was called until an adult, did not read until he was twelve, and it is now generally assumed that he suffered from dyslexia. He overcame it, however, with a grim determination, and soon caught up

6

with his contemporaries. Indeed, he began to show astonishing aptitudes; for example, his boyhood game of inventing navies, with remarkably accurate drawings (though he had never been to a seaport), showed that he knew every class and type of sailing vessel and the use of every sail, shroud, and spar.

Many historians have assumed that Wilson's health was frail in his youth, but Dr. Edwin A. Weinstein, author of *Woodrow Wilson, a Medical and Psychological Biography*, maintains that he was basically healthy, that he was strong and rode horses and played baseball, and that his ailments were psychosomatic: that his headaches and digestive upsets, and even his reluctance to engage in new experiences, were attributable to his mother. Jessie Wilson, according to Weinstein, was a lonely, fearful, discontented woman who prolonged her son's attachment behavior into his adulthood by her overprotectiveness and manipulation of her own ill health and depressions to keep him with her. It was this that made him come home after only a year at Davidson College (near Charlotte, North Carolina) and write in his journal: "I am now in my seventeenth year, and it is sad, when looking over my past life, to see how few of those seventeen years I have spent in the fear of God and how much I have spent in the service of the Devil."

Davidson was a small Presbyterian college aimed particularly at training young men for the ministry, where the living was simple, almost primitive, and the thinking was high. It had probably been chosen by Dr. Wilson because he was one of its trustees and may very naturally have hoped that his serious and devout son would follow his calling. But Wilson, perhaps curiously, never showed any inclination for the church, and after a rather disconsolate period at home following his abandonment of Davidson, he appears to have mastered what Dr. Weinstein calls his "attachment behavior," for after his matriculation at Princeton he stayed the course successfully until his graduation in 1879.

Princeton, or the College of New Jersey, as it was then still called, was a much more sophisticated institution than Davidson, but it was still a small denominational (Presbyterian) school with only five hundred undergraduates and free tuition for the sons of pastors, which may have been one of its attractions to Dr. Wilson. But it was already on its way to become something much more important in the field of education and was attracting the sons of old and established families who had less than no interest in becoming robed mentors. Indeed, the place was having some trouble with rowdy students. Wilson, however, loved it all. He took an active part in undergraduate activities, organizing the Liberal Debating Club, becoming managing editor of the *Princetonian* and president of the Baseball Association, and even having a paper called "Cabinet Government in the United States" published in a Boston review. Though many of his classmates found him cool and standoffish, he made some close friends. Twenty years later he wrote:

Plenty of people offer me their friendship; but partly because I am reserved and shy, and partly because I am fastidious and have a narrow, uncatholic taste in friends,

8

I reject the offer in almost every case—and then am dismayed to look about and see how few persons in the world stand near me and know me as I am.

There has always been some disagreement about Wilson's looks. It has seemed to this writer that the photographs and portraits show a handsome man, with a tall slender face and a tall thin body, a high, noble brow, gravely staring eyes, and a firm, perhaps too firm, jaw. But there were many, including himself, who regarded him as on the homely side, though his admirers professed to see in this the homeliness of a Lincoln. All observers, at any rate, agree that he was impressive. And all agree that he was from his college days a wonderful speaker, one who enunciated clearly and crisply and never seemed to have to grope for a word. How he came by his oratorical gift we do not know, but his father, whom he adored and admired, was a famous preacher.

At some point in his college career he gave up all idea of becoming a minister, nor does his approving and benevolent father seem to have had any objection to his eventual decision to become an attorney. At the University of Virginia Law School he was enthralled by the lectures of the famous John B. Minor, whom he regarded as the greatest teacher he ever had, but his interest in the details of the practice of his profession was as slight as his fascination with its theory was keen. He decided, nonetheless, to hang out his shingle, and he and a Virginia classmate, Edward L. Renick, formed a partnership in Atlanta, Georgia, to whose bar he had been admitted. There followed a year of client-less boredom before he decided to abandon the law. He had always been almost exclusively interested in government and political science, and he had wrongly decided that the practice of law would be his best entry into the field. As he explained in a letter at the time:

> I left college on the wrong tack. I had then, as I have still, a very earnest political creed and very pronounced political ambitions. I remember forming with Charlie Talcott a solemn covenant that we would school our powers and passions for the work of establishing the principles we held in common; that we would acquire knowledge that we might have power; and that we would drill ourselves in all the arts of persuasion but especially in oratory . . . that we might have facility in leading others into our ways of thinking and enlisting them in our purposes.

When he left college he was twenty-one. The above quotation sounds a bit smug, but youth is the time of smug-ness. What is remarkable in Wilson at this age is his confidence that his imagined mission in life was to be carried out through the intellect, and the intellect alone, in an era when the future seemed to belong to the doers rather than the thinkers: the pioneers of the West, the transportation magnates who were covering the land with rails, even the soldiers, like Grant and Hayes and Garfield, who became presidents. Yet Wilson seemed sure that, even without money or political connections or business acumen, he could approach power and influence through academe. His initiation as a statesman was more in the library than in any public forum. His precedent is more to be found in Europe than in America, more in the example of some young priest like the seventeenth-century Richelieu dreaming in the cloister of how he might take over the power of the state from the clumsy military minds that had ruled it so long.

He now enrolled, supported as always by a generous father, as a student in the graduate school of Johns Hopkins University in Baltimore, where he took courses in history, politics, and economics. His ambition, as he expressed it boldly, was "to become an invigorating and enlightening power in the world of political thought."

Graduate school was not the only major change in his life. On a visit to relatives in Rome, Georgia, he had met and fallen in love with the girl he was to marry, Ellen Axson, like his mother and himself the child of a Presbyterian minister. Wilson, as Dr. Weinstein put it, was all his life to need the close companionship of women, preferably adoring and uncritical women, and Ellen "made reality out of the rhetoric by which he idealized" her sex. She gave him a better self "free of his mother's gloom, apprehension and bitterness."

Their economic situation mandated a long engagement, and Wilson wrote passionate letters to his beloved. "I am sometimes absolutely frightened by the intensity of my love for you," he declared. And here is how, with something less than gallantry, he explained away a past infatuation

for his first cousin, Harriet Woodrow, to whom he had unsuccessfully proposed marriage while a law student in
Charlottesville:

> . . . if it was love that I felt for the character which I
> supposed that lady to possess, it was a very con-
> temptible dwarf beside the strong passion that is now at
> large in my heart and which leaps with such tremen-
> dous throbs of joy at the thought of your love.

They were married in June of 1885, and that fall Wilson
took up his first paying job as a professor of history at Bryn
Mawr, a women's college in Pennsylvania. Ellen was a cultivated and well-educated woman, a talented amateur painter
and a poetry lover, with a fine mind that she nonetheless
subjugated to her husband's. The marriage was a happy one,
with one dark episode to be taken up later, lasting until
Ellen's death in 1915, but there may be a question as to
whether the uncritical adulation that she and her three
daughters—Margaret; Jessie (later Mrs. Francis B. Sayre);
and Eleanor (later Mrs. William G. McAdoo)—lavished on
their husband and father was what was really needed by a
nature already too prone to construe disagreement as personal hostility.

The year 1885 was also marked by the publication of
Wilson's most esteemed book, *Congressional Government*,
which brought him something like a national renown, at
least in academic circles. His thesis was that the American
system, in which the business of legislation was carried on

behind closed doors by standing committees of the House and Senate, carried nothing like the efficiency or responsibility to the public of the British system, where the leader of the majority party, as prime minister, selects his cabinet entirely from Parliament and presents his legislative program directly to it. The executive branch, Wilson argued, had atrophied to something approaching powerlessness. The time was coming, however, when the problem so defined would be largely solved by the aggressive leadership of Theodore Roosevelt, in whose steps as a progressive Wilson himself would follow.

Wilson's attraction to the British system may be explained by what had happened politically in America since the Civil War. Starting with the seizure of power by a Congress determined to discipline the defeated South despite all that a depreciated president like Andrew Johnson could do, the chief of state had been largely ignored as a national leader. Grant had the needed popularity, but he was bored and inept in nonmilitary matters and left his government to incompetent and dishonest men. Hayes and Arthur were lightweight statesmen. It is difficult for a large and heterogeneous body of lawmakers to govern a country by the passage of statutes without an executive to organize a majority of them behind some kind of cohesive economic or political plan, and the true governance of America slipped by default, for better and often for worse, into the hands of the business tycoons who controlled our rails, oil, and steel, and, of course, our banking. The time was on its way when

J. P. Morgan would treat with a president almost on equal terms. Small wonder that Wilson should have looked across the Atlantic for a solution to national problems.

Wilson at Johns Hopkins and at Bryn Mawr was at last beginning to have doubts as to whether he would be able to implement his youthful ambition to become a political leader through academe alone. One is surprised they had not come earlier. Was the rough-and-tumble of elections and party rule really consistent with the idealistic thinking of the political scientist? Might he not have to content himself with the indirect influencing of public events through his writing?

He had voiced his early fears in a letter to Ellen in 1884:

> The whole effort of university life is to make men interested in books and in the remote interests which books discuss. . . . And it is this spirit against which I struggle. I want to be near the world; I want to know the world, to retain all my sympathies with it—even with its crudenesses. I am afraid of being a mere student. I want to be a part of the nature around me, not an outside observer of it. . . . Disraeli knew nothing about the true principles of politics, but he knew men—especially House of Commons men. . . . You'll never find in a cloister a fulcrum for any lever which can budge the world.

As yet he could not see his way clear to doing anything but teaching and writing. He had a family now to support, and his college salary was barely enough for that. So he wrote books, as he liked to put it, "for the great host who

14

don't wear spectacles." Sometimes he let his standards drop for a sizable advance. From 1892 to 1902, in addition to his academic duties, he published nine volumes and thirty-five articles and delivered more than twenty public addresses. But if *Congressional Government, Constitutional Government in the United States,* and *Division and Reunion* were shining lights, his five-volume *History of the American People* and his life of George Washington reveal, in the language of even so devoted a Wilson admirer as August Heckscher, "lazy scholarship and a cloying style." Heckscher's life of Wilson, published in 1991 after a near lifetime of study of his subject, is probably the nearest we have come to a definitive biography.

Wilson remained at Bryn Mawr for only three years, leaving it to join the faculty of Wesleyan University in Middletown, Connecticut, as professor of history and political science. He had not been wholly happy at Bryn Mawr, and its trustees felt with some bitterness, though probably wrongly, that he had breached his contractual obligations in departing. In any event, he had not believed that teaching Greek and Roman history to young women—though he conceded that they were alert and attentive—would do much to further his ambition "to add something to the statesmanship of the country, if that something is only thought." Ellen went further; she was afraid that teaching women might actually demean him.

It seems there was always a bit of the Victorian male in Wilson's attitude toward the other sex. Women, he wrote, "have mental and moral gifts of a sort and of a perfection that men lack, but they have not the same gifts that men have. Their life must supplement men's life." And he once referred to "the chilled, scandalized feeling that always comes over me when I see and hear women speak in public."

At Wesleyan, where he remained for the next two years, he was much more popular and successful, and we begin to get our first impression of the dynamic figure who would hold vast crowds in awe with his oratory and idealism. His students' comments were enthusiastic: "He had a contagious interest—his eyes flashed." "I can see him now, with his hands forward, the tips of his fingers just touching the table, his face earnest and animated." "He talked to us in the most informed, jolly way, yet with absolute clearness and sureness." Wilson also organized "the Wesleyan House of Commons," a debating society based on the British Parliament, which became a center of undergraduate activity, and served on a two-man advisory board to coach the football team.

In the fall of 1890 he commenced his duties at Princeton in the Chair of Jurisprudence and Political Economy, which he held until his election as president of the university in 1902. This was probably the happiest period of his life. There are fewer reports of his "cool" personality, and some of his faculty friendships were intimate. The undergraduates voted him their most popular professor year after year, and it was reported that some of his classes applauded and even stamped their feet at the close of a lecture. His home life was happy, and his big house was always full, for he was unfailingly hospitable to his and Ellen's poor relations. At family gatherings he was known for his comic impersonations: the drunken man staggering about with a cowlike look in his eyes, the heavy Englishman with an insufferably superior accent and an invisible monocle, the villain done with a scowl and a dragging foot.

But a new era began when he was elevated to the presidency. He had attained a national reputation with his writings and speeches, and he was now head of a university that was determined to rival Yale and Harvard. Was there still time and occasion for him to enter the political field that he had dreamed of as a youth? He was forty-five. We find this note in his papers: "I was born a politician and must be at the task, for which, by means of my historical writing, I have all these years been in training."

As fortune would have it, just at the moment, in the fall of 1902, when Wilson was contemplating a future in politics, the man who was to first launch him on his way to the White House attended his inauguration at Princeton and was inspired by his address to go home and read all his books. Colonel George B. M. Harvey now dared to hope that he had discovered the man who could rescue the Democratic Party from the disastrous leadership of William Jennings Bryan!

Harvey was a New York journalist who had risen to the managing editorship of the *World* under the auspices of Joseph Pulitzer. He had also, associated with Thomas Fortune Ryan, made a fortune in public utilities, which had enabled him to buy the *North American Review* and become editor of Harper and Brothers and *Harper's Weekly*. It was he who, in 1904, would induce the novelist Henry James to revisit his native land after twenty years in Europe by offering to publish his account of his travels. He would meet the shy and stammering author of *The Golden Bowl* at the dock and sweep him off for a night at his mansion in Deal, New Jersey, terrifying him with the threat of a huge public tributory dinner which the captive writer protested he would flee to "Arizona or Alaska" to avoid! To James the "objectionable colonel" was the essence of the ebullient, hustling, intruding, publicity-loving new America that he was to deplore in *The American Scene*, which Harvey did indeed publish. But to hungry Democratic bosses, Harvey, who had now made politics his passionate hobby, was a useful and imaginative kingmaker.

But it would not be until 1910 that he would offer Wilson the governorship of New Jersey, so to speak, on a silver platter. We must deal first with the president of Princeton.

2

————

THE FIRST FIVE YEARS were a resounding success. Wilson was opposed to the Harvard system, introduced in the administration of Charles W. Eliot, of allowing the students freedom to elect any courses they chose, with the result, at least theoretically, that Icelandic sagas might be credited with the same educational value as Shakespeare's tragedies and the history of Abyssinia with that the Roman Empire. Wilson aspired to a broader base; he insisted that undergraduates start with at least one course in each of the four principal divisions of the scholastic curriculum—philosophy, art and archaeology, language and literature, and mathematics and science—and specialize as they progressed.

His most popular innovation, though one for which large sums had to be raised, was the establishment of a preceptorial system. Wilson had long felt that the gulf between faculty and students was too wide, and he hired fifty young teachers, or "preceptors," like the tutors in English colleges, to live on campus with the undergraduates and guide them, or, as he liked to put it, "intellectualize" them. The plan worked well, one reason being that it was heartily backed

19

by the faculty, who saw these preceptors as welcome assistants.

In May of 1906 Wilson suffered a stroke, a blockage of the left ophthalmic artery, which permanently damaged the vision of his left eye. He had undergone a lesser stroke in 1896, an occlusion of a central branch of the left middle cerebral artery, which had caused a temporary loss of dexterity in his right hand. His recovery from both these incidents, except for his eye, had apparently been complete, but Dr. Weinstein believes they may have had a permanent aftereffect in intensifying his natural irritability and stubbornness. Of course, there has been endless speculation as to what effect these and later strokes may have had on Wilson's capacity as the nation's chief executive and, in particular, on his handling of the negotiations leading to the Versailles Treaty.

In 1907 Ellen sent Wilson on a vacation alone to Bermuda to recover his health while she stayed with the children, and there he met Mary Allen Hulbert Peck. An attractive, bright, sympathetic woman six years his junior, she was separated from her second husband and had taken a large house on the island in which she loved to entertain notables, to distract her, perhaps, from her constant money troubles. Dr. Weinstein suggests that she was "a histrionic, self-indulgent, flirtatious woman, dependent on the pleasures of society and the attentions of important men," but Wilson was fascinated by her, missed her desperately on a second trip to Bermuda, kept up with her through the years, lent her money, and corresponded with her for the rest of his life.

He even tried to explain her to Ellen! When she taxed him once by letter with this "emotional love," he replied:

"Emotional love!"—ah, dearest, that was a cutting and cruel judgment and utterly false, and as natural as false, but I never blamed you for it or wondered at it. I only understand—only saw the thing as you see it and as it is *not*, and suffered, am suffering still, ah, how deeply!— but with access of love, constant access of love. My darling! I have never been worthy of you, but I love you with all my poor, mixed inexplicable nature and everything fine and tender in me.

August Heckscher ascribes this rather bizarre outpouring to Wilson's double nature:

These complex relationships show the dualism that often characterized Wilson. He could appear to be two different men, the one scarcely aware of what the other was thinking. Thus he seems never to have felt the need to make a choice between his wife and Mary Peck. The same post that in 1909 carried from Bermuda letters to Ellen that might have been those of a bridegroom to a bride, carried to Mary passionate assurances of how ardently she was missed.

Yet Heckscher believes that in 1910, in New York City, Wilson and Peck had an actual affair. And it is certainly true that Ellen, at the end of her life, confided to Cary Grayson that the Peck matter was the only unhappiness that her husband had caused her during their entire marriage. And when Wilson, as a widower, was purporting to make a clean breast of the business to his new love interest, Edith Bolling Galt, he wrote that he came to her under the burden of "a folly long ago loathed and repented of" and that he stood before her "stained and unworthy." Finally, as evidence of his vulnerability to sexual temptation, there is his curious admission to Ellen, in the early years of their marriage, that when he went to New York from Princeton to give a course at New York Law School, he dared not stay overnight because of what his "imperious passions" might drive him to do. Ellen had answered that she was sure that "nothing dreadful would have happened." Perhaps she was right. Who knows?

The concept of the two Wilsons may help to explain the two great crises of his Princeton career; the first of these crises rocked his presidency, and on the second it foundered. They were the quadrangle plan and the location of the graduate school.

Social life among the undergraduates centered around the eating clubs, and as these could not—and had no desire to—include all of the student body, large numbers of students were left out, and made to feel, presumably, that they were not a true part of the "real" Princeton. Such a system inevitably fostered every kind of social snobbery, and Wilson hated it. Even toward the end of his life he was still saying: "Princeton is exactly what they say of it: a fine country club, where many of the alumni make snobs of their boys." As John Milton Cooper aptly expressed it: Wilson's "symbolic antagonist was a boy who did not enter Princeton until three years after Wilson left—F. Scott Fitzgerald." The "beautiful and damned" in American youth were more damned in Wilson's eyes than in those of Gatsby's creator.

The quadrangle plan that he endorsed would have established a number of residential colleges where all undergraduates would have to live and board. It was a plan later adopted by Harvard and Yale and, ultimately, by Princeton itself. It was not aimed specifically at the eating clubs, but it would obviously hurt them, as their members might have to pay for two sets of meals.

The opposition to the plan was both strong and well organized, bolstered by many important alumni, including Wilson's great friend and backer, the wealthy Moses Taylor Pyne, and Wilson went down to a crushing defeat. He did not take it well, and here again we are confronted with the dual nature of his personality. One side was that of the sensible and sensitive man of many interests and activities who conscientiously viewed all sides of a question. The other was that of the self-assured idealist who could hardly conceive, much less admit, that he could be wrong in judging matters that he deemed within his peculiar sphere of expertise: the education of young men, the upholding of moral values, and, as we shall see, the establishment of world peace. This Wilson, with God and his angels presumably ranked behind him, tended to regard opposition as malicious betrayal. Alas, it was a Wilson whose nature seemed to be aggravated by the ill health that was increasingly to dog him. Small wonder that the opponents of his college plan were surprised and at last angered to see the dynamic and forceful university president whose ringing speeches had electrified alumni gatherings and college commencements across the nation turn into the bitter and disillusioned man who broke even with intimate friends whose consciences required them to disagree with him.

The Wilson of the better side sought at first to save his friendship, the closest he had ever had, with John Grier Hibben, a professor of philosophy, and wrote to him: "And our friendship, by which I have lived, in which I have drawn some of the most refreshing, most renewing breath of my life, is to be as little defeated by our difference of opinion as is everything permanent and of the law of our hearts."

But he found himself unable to sustain this lofty attitude. He turned his back on Hibben at last and never received him as a friend again.

The second crisis exploded with the question of whether the new graduate school should be located off campus in the country, a condition attached to the proposed funding of a rich sponsor, or amalgamated with the rest of the university buildings. Andrew W. West, the dean, and a formidably aggressive adversary, wished to have his students isolated from noisy undergraduates in a quiet sylvan atmosphere that he could solemnly dominate; Wilson insisted that all members of the college and graduate schools would profit from the mutual exchanges in joint search for knowledge. The battle raged rancorously until another rich sponsor died leaving purported millions to the West plan.

Wilson had to recognize a second defeat. "We can beat the living," he said ruefully, "but we cannot fight the dead."

Wilson now did what he would do again and again when his way was crossed: appeal to what he hoped would be the greater and more favorable court of public opinion. As he would plead futilely for the League of Nations to the American public after its rejection by the Senate, so did he now travel to different cities in search of alumni support. In Pittsburgh, in 1910, he uttered these intemperate words. His reference to France was probably inspired by the denunciations of the excesses of the 1789 Revolution by Edmund Burke, whose principles he greatly admired.

> The great voice of America does not come from the seats of learning but in a murmur from the hills and the woods and the farms and the factories and the mills, rolling on and gaining volume until it comes to us the voice from the homes of the common man. . . . If she loses her self-possession America will stagger like France through fields of blood before she finds peace and prosperity under the leadership of men who understand her needs.

If we find it hard at times to understand the two sides of Wilson's nature, it may be helpful to remember that he had the same difficulty.

3

COLONEL HARVEY, with his offer to Wilson of the Democratic nomination for the governorship of New Jersey, became the deus ex machina of the graduate school tragedy. For Wilson, true to his faith in the British cabinet system, had felt that, like a prime minister who has lost a vote of confidence, he should resign his office as president. Ellen, for once, took a strong and positive position in the matter, pointing out that he need not resign, since Harvey's offer "sets you free again to leave if you wish—that is to accept the nomination for governor and going into politics."

Colonel Harvey was essentially a New Yorker, but he had a home in New Jersey, and he had cultivated close relations with James Smith and his nephew, James Nugent, the Democratic bosses of Newark and of Essex County, the most populous in the state. Smith was a portly gentleman, suave, poised, affable, wealthy and self-made, who had been a United States senator and looked forward to being one again. He and Harvey had plans and ambitions that went far beyond state borders; they looked for nothing less than to put a man of their choice in the White House (as Theodore Roosevelt had recently renamed the executive mansion), toward which the gubernatorial office in Trenton was only a stepping-stone. As early as 1906 Harvey had placed on the top of each issue of *Harper's Weekly:* "Woodrow Wilson for President." Looking forward to the national election in 1912, he and Smith saw Taft as the Republican candidate, but did not underestimate Roosevelt, who now notoriously detested the man he had chosen to be his successor, and might make a strong bid for a third term. And whom did the Democrats have? The silver-tongued advocate of free silver, William Jennings Bryan, a three times presidential loser, couldn't be run again. They needed a new face.

Harvey was closely allied to big-business interests in New York, and big business and boss politics had long formed an unholy alliance. Smith wanted a governor and Harvey a president who wasn't going to rock their boats, but to stand any chance of defeating Roosevelt's Progressives, they would need a man of liberal inclinations, at least in his public pronouncements, and preferably one who, unsophisticated in the murky dealings of boss politics, would be guided by such friendly smooth talkers as themselves. In short, they needed a man who *looked* like a liberal, and who better fitted that role than an innocent, renowned, and unimpeachably honest academic?

But what made two such sharp and practiced men of the world imagine that a man of Wilson's strong and contentious personality was the candidate they sought? To understand this, one must turn to some of Wilson's earlier and lesser-known statements. He had certainly been at one point in his life an economic conservative. He had stated his view that he did not, like Roosevelt, believe in governmental regulation of the trusts, but simply that the attorney general should be swift to penalize them when and if they stepped over the line of the law. "We cannot abolish the trusts," he asserted; "we must moralize them." And where labor unions were concerned he had said that government should guarantee to every worker the right to sell his labor as he pleased for the price he was willing to accept. Could Henry Clay Frick have asked for more? Wilson had even once praised Tammany Hall for its effectiveness! Worse still, in his *History of the American People* he had drawn an offensive picture of illiterate and unclean Hungarian and Polish immigrants, concluding that "the Chinese were more to be desired as workmen if not as citizens than most of the coarse crew that come crowding in every year at the eastern ports."

What had happened, apparently unbeknownst to the Colonel, was that from 1908 to 1910 Wilson had been moving steadily to the left. It is hard not to speculate that the rough treatment he had received from the wealthy graduates of Princeton and his growing disgust with the country-club atmosphere created in the college by the sons of privilege had awakened him to the dangers of a society of too much money and power concentrated in the hands of too few. All his life he was to be to some extent like Justice Holmes, a distruster of political absolutes and sweeping government intervention in the affairs of men, but, as would soon enough be seen, that left plenty of room for legislative programs highly distasteful to his original backers. Harvey should have noted the tone of the 1910 address to the Pittsburgh alumni already quoted.

The great twentieth-century issues between economic conservatives and liberals—what powers should labor unions enjoy, what controls should muzzle business, and what public relief should the federal government grant—were just beginning to be defined. Liberals were starting to speculate that the Commerce Clause of the Constitution might open up fields of corporate regulation hitherto undreamed of, while conservatives were passionately maintaining that the Fourteenth Amendment exempted companies from legislative interference in precisely the same way it did individuals. Wilson, as we shall see, did not believe that the Constitution even allowed the federal government to proscribe labor for children of any age, and a majority of the voters seem to have agreed with him. So the real issue between a liberal and a conservative in a state election at this time was how a candidate stood on boss rule, and even this was not clear, as it was almost as necessary for *any* candidate to depreciate the bosses as it was for a clergyman to denounce sin. Thus, the true issue was whether or not a voter believed in the candidate's sincerity. All of which may help to explain why Colonel Harvey and his friends were deceived in the man they put forward.

Wilson was offered the nomination—or rather the political support that seemed to guarantee it—without any pledges and without his even lifting a hand, and he promptly accepted the offer, resigning his post at Princeton.

The backing given him at the Democratic state convention as a little-known (by the delegates, anyway) professor, and apparent tool of the bosses, was, to say the least, lukewarm, but it was just enough to ensure his nomination. Wilson's acceptance speech, however, changed the whole picture. He was and always would be a splendid orator. His stout assertion: "I did not seek this nomination. It has come to me absolutely unsolicited," followed in emphatic tones by the assurance that he was under no pledge of any kind, caused the convention to erupt in wild cheers. Delegate Joseph P. Tumulty, a forward-looking young assemblyman who had regarded Wilson as the puppet of reactionaries, was converted on the spot and threw in his lot wholeheartedly with this new star whose secretary he would become and remain through all the years. He was later in a memoir about his chief to describe the dramatic and historic sight at this convention of "all the old guard moving with Prussian precision to the nomination of the man who was to destroy for a time the machine rule in New Jersey and inaugurate a new national era in political liberalism, while all the liberal elements of the state including . . . young men like myself were sullen, helpless."

In the gubernatorial campaign Wilson continued to strike his loud, clear note of independence from the party machine. In a public letter exchange with George L. Record, a Republican congressional candidate who challenged him on the boss issue, he had the chance to assert ringingly: "I should deem myself forever disgraced should I

LOUIS AUCHINCLOSS

ever in the slightest degree cooperate in any such system or any such transactions as you describe in your characterization of the 'boss' system."

Record remarked when he heard this: "That letter will elect Wilson governor."

Whether or not it was the letter, he won a sweeping victory, polling twice the votes of his adversary.

As governor-elect Wilson did not wait for his inauguration before crossing swords with James Smith, the boss of Newark. Elections for the United States Senate in New Jersey were still made by the legislature. At a state senatorial Democratic primary a political nobody, James E. Martine, had been nominated, and it was expected that he would simply withdraw when the great Mr. Smith, who had not at the time of the convention made up his mind to run, decided at last to do so. But Wilson resolved to take up the cudgels for Martine, who after a bitter fight in the legislature was duly elected senator, a position that he maintained with more dignity and effectiveness than had been anticipated. Smith, with bemusement, regarded Wilson as a puzzling traitor, but his nephew, Nugent, at a private party, proposed a toast to "the Governor of New Jersey, an ingrate and a liar." This bit of bravado cost him his post as chairman of the state Democratic committee. Bossism in the cities had received a definite setback.

As governor, Wilson implemented his theory of modeling the chief executive on the British prime minister and took an active role in personally presenting his legislative

32

program to the state assembly and senate and arguing its
merits. He continued his fight against the political machinery that dominated the cities by the establishment of com-
missions for urban rule, and he obtained the passage of a
corrupt-practices law mandating direct party primary nom-
inations of all delegates to national conventions, requiring
candidates for the legislature to state if they would support
the senatorial candidate endorsed at the party primary, directing personal registration of voters, and ordering the
mailing of sample ballots to voters before a general election.
He also obtained the enactment of a workmen's compensa-
tion law and the establishment of a public utilities commission to regulate rates and services.

But for all his success in public office, the abandonment
of the shades of academe (despite the vicious struggles they
concealed) had not come easily to Wilson. His naïveté
about campaign expenses had been vividly illustrated to the
bosses by his initial assumption that he could pay them personally, as they shouldn't exceed five hundred dollars! Of
course, the politicians ended by spending a hundred times
that figure. And he found it difficult to maintain constantly
the democratic grin and affable mien expected of a governor. In his sober Trenton office, lined with law books and
the stern portraits of former governors, he would dictate as
many as a hundred letters in a morning, many at the urging
of Tumulty for obvious political reasons, and stare out the
window at the muddy Delaware, feeling, as he put it, "like a
wild bird in a cage." He tried to use a Dictaphone but gave

it up, discouraged by the odd sound of his own voice. Only in the evening did he have a chance to put his thoughts and ideas together.

Yet even the evenings were not ideal. His family had to put up with the cramped suite that the state had taken for its governor in the Princeton Inn, unless it was summertime and they had the use of the stuffy cottage in Sea Bright on the shore, where they could watch from the piazza the marching soldiers on the parade ground of a military station next door. There had been the possible distraction of a nude Narcissus statue in the front hall, but public prudery had caused it to be removed from a public building. Poor Ellen disliked having no household duties, but she was, as always, a good sport, and the girls were for the most part away, engaged in their various pursuits of music, painting, and social work.

By the middle of his term, anyway, Wilson had added the fame of a vigorous and liberal governor to his already established reputation as a noted political scientist, and it was clear that he would be a serious candidate for the Democratic presidential nomination in the 1912 Baltimore convention. His antiboss stand and, more important, his implementation of it in office, could be pitted against Roosevelt's Progressive Republicans, even if the latter formed a third party. He was a scholar and an idealist who at the same time had proven that he could win an election; he was a splendid speaker, and he *looked* like a president, tall and straight and serious. It was also not to be overlooked that he was a southerner by birth and raising and that the South had not had a president since the Civil War and was certainly due one.

In November of 1911 Wilson met the man who was to become his most intimate friend and constant counselor. Colonel Edward M. House (the title was honorary, bestowed by a grateful Texas governor) was a southerner transplanted to New York who had plenty of money and time and brains to devote to his passionate behind-the-scenes hobby of advising politicians. His dream was to find a candidate to defeat Taft or Roosevelt in 1912, and as he knew Colonel Harvey—indeed he made it his business to know everybody—his path soon crossed Wilson's. The two men were physically almost opposites: Wilson was tall and impressive as a statesman and orator whereas House was short and frail, with a receding chin and a voice that lacked resonance. But something extraordinary at once clicked between them. "We have known each other always," Wilson wrote him. And later, in 1913, when House was firmly ensconced as a White House adviser (though he never, until the peace treaty negotiations in 1919, had any salary or title), Wilson made this remarkable statement to a politician:

> Mr. House is my second personality. He is my independent self. If I were in his place I would do just as he suggested. If anyone thinks he is reflecting my opinion by whatever action he takes, they are welcome to the conclusion.

Now this is an exceptional statement for any man, let alone a president of the United States, to make. The trouble with famous friendships or partnerships in history is that many chroniclers tend to feel that they must take sides with one friend or the other, particularly if there is an ultimate break, as was the case with Wilson and House. Did Harry Hopkins dominate the ailing FDR? Was Queen Elizabeth I a fretful puppet in the hands of Burghley? Was Father Joseph the real power behind Richelieu?

The private papers of Colonel House published after Wilson's death irritated many of the president's admirers because House seems at times to condescend to his friend as less mentally equipped than his adviser to make the great decisions, and to imply that a goodly part of anything that was beneficial to the world in Wilson's government came from House's untiring manipulation of the presidential mind. But House's egotism and conceit—even if we call them that—are not the final word on what he contributed or failed to contribute to Wilson's decisions and acts.

To my thinking, Walter Lippmann, who had one of the clearest and most encompassing minds of his era and who knew Wilson well and House better (they worked closely together in the war, preparing for peace), has made the most significant of all the evaluations of the relationship between the two men. Lippmann believed that House, because he remained in communication with men who bored or angered or simply disagreed with Wilson, and because he lacked Wilson's fierce conviction about ideas, and because he had broader sympathies with ordinary human beings, was able to save the president's administration from the

sectarian narrowness of dedicated reformers and make it
broadly national in spirit.

> The Colonel kept open the channels of understanding
> between the solitary man in the White House and the
> representatives of all sorts of indispensable and influen-
> tial men. He kept open the channels with the practical
> politicians of the Democratic party, men who spoke the
> language that the President could read but could not
> speak fluently. He kept open the channels with the par-
> ties on the left, with pacifists and socialists and single-
> minded reformers, whom a president in those days
> could easily have forgotten about. With equal dexterity
> he kept open the channels of communication with big
> business and high finance, and with Republican leaders
> like Mr. Taft and Mr. Root. And, as everyone knows, he
> made personal contact with the leading personalities of
> Germany, France and Great Britain.

House thus brought to Wilson the one great faculty that
he lacked: the faculty of dealing with a huge variety of different human beings. Fortunately, Lippmann concludes,
Wilson knew his own weakness, "and fortunately he found
in Colonel House a man whom he was able to see often
without becoming weary, a man whom he trusted and
knew to be sensitive and responsive to the things he cared
about."

Lippmann has shown us what Wilson had to gain from
the friendship; we may ask what there was in it for House.
It had to be the only way the latter could imagine of fulfill-

ing an ambition so great, as he put it in his autobiography, that it had never seemed worth his while to try to satisfy it. House wanted nothing less than to induce the nations of the world to beat their swords into plowshares and establish universal concord. Handicapped from youth by poor health, unimpressive physically, ill-equipped for oratory or leadership, he needed a force *through* which he could use all his subtlety and brilliance, and in Wilson he at once found his man. But he was always conscious of the fact that too much public recognition of his influence might arouse the jealousy of even the most benevolent chief, and he invariably played down the significance of his role to the White House circle and particularly to the press, whom he handled with consummate skill, attributing the credit of every action to the president whose humble servant he was.

Yet inevitably there was much public curiosity about this mystery man behind the scenes. Once, when Wilson and House were attending divine services together, the minister, to House's consternation, offered a prayer for "our president and his counsellor." Still, despite all the pundits and columns and queries, the relationship remained in force for eight long years.

It was, in short, a remarkable case of symbiosis, two organisms in a close contact beneficent to each, each supplementing the needs of the other. And so it lasted until it was broken up by two factors: the bitter jealousy of the second Mrs. Wilson, who wished to substitute her own advice and influence for House's, and the acceptance by House of his first official position in the Peace Commission, which fatally altered his formerly unique place in the president's heart and mind.

Coming back to August Heckscher's concept of the two Woodrow Wilsons, is it possible that Wilson himself was dimly aware of this, and that some kind of instinctual intuition operated in his early meetings with House to make him recognize that here at last was just the man to restrain and moderate the stubborn and self-pitying side of his own personality? Probably not. It is more likely that House was primarily responsible for their immediate rapport. He described in his journal a conversation that he had with Wilson about their first encounter:

> I asked if he remembered the first day we met, some three and a half years ago. He replied, "Yes, but we had known one another always, and merely came in touch then, for our purposes and thoughts were one." I told him how much he had been to me; how I had tried all my life to find someone with whom I could work out the things I had so deeply at heart, and I had begun to despair, believing my life should be more or less a failure, when he came into it, giving me the opportunity for which I had been longing.

4

PROBABLY THE LAST THING that the American man in the street would have suspected in 1912 was that in two years' time an incident in the Balkans would set off a world war in which two million of his fellow countrymen would have to fight. The drama that then most concerned our newspaper readers was Theodore Roosevelt's break with President William Howard Taft and the split of the Republican Party, which had so long dominated the nation. Roosevelt had enjoyed a popularity at home and abroad accorded to no other American chief of state, and he had come to think of himself as indispensable to his nation's welfare. But when his near megalomania caused him to refer publicly to his own—as opposed to the voters'—selection of his successor, by chastising Taft for biting the hand that fed him, a profound shock was caused. The division of the Republicans assured a Democratic victory at the polls, and indeed the final result gave Wilson a popular vote of some 6,300,000, with 4,125,000 for Roosevelt and 3,500,000 for Taft.

Perhaps the most significant aspect of the election was the swing to the left. Obviously, there was profound discontent at the way things were, and a growing feeling that big business was too sorely grinding the poor. Roosevelt in office had done some trust-busting, to be sure, but this had not nearly solved the problem, and Taft had been a known friend of Wall Street. The Socialist Party polled more votes than ever before in its history, and large numbers of Roosevelt's Progressives opted for Wilson.

House did not play an important part in the 1912 campaign; he did not even attend the Baltimore convention. He dreaded the effect of hot weather on his frail health—it would be the only thing in the next eight years that would ever interfere with his duty to Wilson—and Baltimore was broiling. The three most important Wilson backers were Walter H. Page, the brilliant journalist who became editor in chief of Doubleday Page and Company and whom Wilson was to make the too fervently Anglophile ambassador to Great Britain; William F. McCombs, chairman of the Democratic Party, an astute and able manipulator of politicians but a sick man, moody, hypersensitive and irritable, and very much out of step with the progressive side of his party, whom Wilson reluctantly but loyally kept in his position after the election until his health gave out; and William G. McAdoo, a capable and dominating southerner who had made a fortune in New York building a tube under the Hudson River before entering politics with a hearty lust for power, and who was to become Wilson's secretary of the treasury and son-in-law without ever winning Wilson's unreserved affection.

McCombs and McAdoo handled the convention astutely; to them, perhaps, more than to any others, Wilson owed his nomination. The prime contender and apparent favorite was James B. "Champ" Clark of Missouri, Speaker of the House of Representatives, who was backed by the powerful Bryan, whom Wilson had antagonized by a private letter, unhappily publicized, in which he had expressed the hope that some way might be found, "at once dignified and effective," to knock Bryan "once and for all into a cocked hat." Fortunately Bryan was not a petty man, and when, distressed by Tammany Hall's noisy endorsement of Clark, he shifted his delegates to Wilson, the battle was over, and news of his nomination was brought to the latter in Sea Bright, where he was patiently expecting defeat, quite resigned to God's evident disapproval of his candidacy.

The candidate, now undertaking the campaign, proved a good deal more fiery and more liberal than his sponsors had expected. Toward the end of his gubernatorial term, Wilson had been showing himself more of a progressive. Addressing a group of bankers in New York City he had stated flatly that they took no interest in the small depositor. The mighty Morgan, listening glumly as he puffed fiercely at his cigar, asked gruffly afterward whether this had been aimed at him, and Wilson coolly denied it. If Harvey had been present, he should have made a note. Perhaps he did, for after the nomination, when Wilson met him at the Manhattan Club in New York, he laid an arm on the candidate's shoulder and asked for a frank answer to his question of whether he thought the endorsement of *Harper's Weekly* would hurt his campaign. Wilson replied that he thought it might, at least in the West. Harvey promptly withdrew his support of the ticket, and Wilson was widely accused of ingratitude, but, after all, it was Harvey who had asked the question.

Wilson, campaigning in San Francisco, sounded almost like Bryan, the Great Commoner:

> Money is at the bottom of all misrepresentation to the people. Not money put into hands—not bribes, that's old-fashioned and crude. The present plan is to convince men that, if they do not do as they are told to do in politics, they can't get money for their business.

Asked by a reporter how he had managed to switch from a cloistered academic life to the political arena, he replied that politicians were "neophytes in the art of intrigue compared with some of these Princeton politicians."

At times he began to sound like an Old Testament prophet:

> I believe that God presided over the inception of this nation. I believe that God planted in us the vision of liberty. I cannot be deprived of the hope that is in me . . . that we are chosen to show the way to the nations of the world how they shall walk in the paths of liberty.

Wilson's oratory, eloquent, impassioned, soaring with moral imperative, had a hypnotic effect on crowds. And regarding the occupation of the Philippines he sounded as belligerent as Roosevelt. The fighting there meant "that this country has young men who prefer dying in the ditches of the Philippines to spending their lives behind the counters of a dry goods store in our eastern cities. I think I should prefer that myself."

McCombs recorded a cool interview after the voting with the president-elect in which the latter gravely assured him that he had no obligations to any politicians no matter what their contribution to his election had been: "I wish it clearly understood that I owe you nothing. Remember that God ordained that I should be the next president of the United States."

Was Thomas Riley Marshall, the vice president in both of Wilson's terms, who is remembered only for his statement that "what this country needs is a good five-cent cigar," also the choice of the Deity?

The new president reflected the national mood of wanting "something to be *done*" in his inaugural address, the shortest to that date in our history. It was the appropriate introduction to the "New Freedom," which came to be the motto of his first term, signifying the country's release from the grip of economic monopolies.

> We have been proud of our industrial achievements, but we have not hitherto stopped thoughtfully enough to count the human cost, the cost of lives snuffed out, of energies overtaxed and broken, the fearful physical and spiritual cost of the men and women and children upon whom the dead weight and burden of it all has fallen pitilessly the years through. The groans and agony of it all had not yet reached our ears, the solemn, moving undertone of our life, coming up out of the mines and fac-

tories and out of every home where the struggle had its intimate and familiar seat. . . . The great government we loved has too often been made use of for private and selfish purposes, and those who used it had forgotten the people. . . . There has been something crude and heartless and unfeeling in our haste to succeed and be great. Our thought has been "Let every man look out for himself," while we reared giant machinery which made it impossible for any but those who stood at the levers of control should have a chance to look out for themselves. . . . This is the high enterprise of the new day: To lift everything that concerns our life as a Nation to the light that shines from the hearthfire of every man's conscience and vision of the right. . . . We shall restore, not destroy.

How did all this differ from Roosevelt's approach to the same problem? Perhaps not too drastically. The two men had liked each other well enough on a first meeting, but two factors turned them into deadly opponents. The first was Wilson's expressed regrets to the Republic of Colombia for the role played by the United States in supporting the Panamanian Revolution in the interests of Roosevelt's Canal policy, and the second was the issue of neutrality in World War I. But domestically they were not far apart. Their differences in the approach to the problem of the trusts, for example, were more in theory than in effect. Roosevelt favored direct governmental control of big business to keep it in line, whereas Wilson, advised by Louis D. Brandeis (whom he later appointed to the Supreme Court), preferred to work through the Federal Trade Commission and use its power to issue cease and desist orders against those that impeded competition. Viewed from the era of the New Deal, when government really muscled into the corporate picture, the distinction seems minor.

A greater resemblance between the two administrations is in the forceful way that the executive took the lead in sponsoring legislation. If the two houses of Congress had been the true rulers of the country in the period between Lincoln's and McKinley's assassinations, there is little question which branch of government held the dominant power under Roosevelt and Wilson. Neither man hesitated to appeal to the nation as its true leader over the heads of Congress. The real distinction between them was one of temperament.

John Milton Cooper has put it this way:

> The difference between them as political intellectuals resembled the Apollonian and Dionysian syntheses of emotional and rational elements in art. Roosevelt, the Dionysian artist, favored the primacy of emotion. Wilson was the Apollonian, favoring the primacy of reason.

But this is subject to a qualification. Cooper cites Roosevelt's emulation of Lincoln, who achieved his objectives of preserving the union and emancipating the slaves by combining eloquent speeches with shrewd politics. And when Roosevelt did this, he knew exactly what he was doing. Wilson also compromised his ideals; indeed, a hostile member of his cabinet, Lindley Garrison, his first secretary of war, described him as a man of high ideals but no principles. Yet when Wilson compromised, he tried very hard to convince himself that he was still acting morally. Roosevelt, as a result, was a man whom even his enemies could love as a man basically honest; Wilson was a man whom his enemies distrusted as a hypocrite. Both, of course, had their worshipers.

As the time came to pick a cabinet, Colonel House was on hand to suggest appointments from his long and carefully researched list. And when Wilson's well-organized mind and rapid grasp of factual situations operated under the soft restraint of House's tactfully presented realism, beneficent results could sometimes ensue.

It was appalling that the insular and pacifist Bryan should be made secretary of state, a job for which he was manifestly unfit, but it was an absolute political necessity. However, Josephus Daniels, editor of the *Raleigh News and Observer*, despite his unconventional views about relaxing the rigid division of naval ranks and his opposition to any drinking on ships, proved an adequate secretary of the navy, particularly when backed up by the assistant secretary, young Franklin D. Roosevelt. The hot-tempered and argumentative Lindley Garrison was chosen for secretary of war, but he ultimately broke with the president and was replaced by Newton D. Baker, a needed and able leader when war came. The atrabilious James C. McReynolds was chosen for attorney general but was soon elevated to the Supreme Court, where he survived to become the remorseless enemy of New Deal legislation, and after an interim appointment, in 1920 the president, distracted by peacemaking in Paris, appointed A. Mitchell Palmer, who stained the administration with his postwar red-baiting. William G. McAdoo was awarded for his services with the Treasury and the hand of Wilson's daughter Eleanor; David Houston, a friend of House's and president of the University of Texas, became secretary of agriculture, a post he held for two terms; Franklin K. Lane, a progressive westerner and former interstate commerce commissioner, was given the Department of the Interior. Albert S. Burleson, an experienced politician and Texan, was postmaster general. Wilson was dissuaded from including Brandeis in the cabinet because he was too liberal.

House even acted for the president in announcing the appointments. Walter Hines Page learned that he had been named ambassador to the United Kingdom from House's cheerful greeting on the telephone: "Good morning, Your Excellency!" And David Houston was not even sure that he should go to Washington. He told Page: "I have never to this good day received any notification of my appointment as Secretary of Agriculture except that which I received from Colonel House." It is interesting to note that Wilson successfully suggested to his rich friend and backer Cleveland Dodge that he give Page twenty-five thousand dollars a year to supplement the inadequate salary of an ambassador.

Wilson presided with a cool dignity at cabinet meetings, asking the members for their opinions with studied good manners. But it was evident that he believed that he could best work out problems alone—or by discussing them with House. He saw to the heart of any question with lightning rapidity and quickly tired of repetitious explanation. He would even delegate House to warn too garrulous cabinet members that they should be briefer.

The new postmaster general, like House, had to open his new chief's eyes to some of the basic realities of the relationship between the White House and Congress, but he did so much more bluntly. When Wilson told him that he wanted all federal appointments to be made on a strict basis of merit, Burleson gave him the facts on patronage: "Mr. President, if you pursue this policy it means that your administration is going to be a failure. . . . It doesn't matter a damn who is postmaster in Paducah, Kentucky. But these little offices mean a great deal to senators and representatives in Congress."

Wilson listened to him, and when he came around to Burleson's point of view, he did so thoroughly, almost too much so. By giving in to Bryan and appointing his political hacks to diplomatic posts that Roosevelt had endeavored to fill with talented men, he did much to lower the prestige and effectiveness of our embassies and consulates all over the world. But he saw that it was necessary to get his legislative program, the so-called New Freedom, through both houses, and this he embarked on with much of Roosevelt's dynamic leadership. Later he was even to admit that some of the conservative congressional "standpatters at least will stand by the party and the administration. I can rely on them better than some of my own crowd." He would soon become expert with the party whip.

Life at the White House was not brilliant socially, as it had been with the Roosevelts. The Wilsons were family-oriented and loved quiet evenings with a few friends where Wilson would read aloud, often from his favorite poets, Wordsworth and Browning. He rose at eight, breakfasted on two raw eggs, oatmeal, and coffee, dictated to his stenographer, Charles Swem (though he sometimes typed himself), from nine to ten, received visitors (only by appointment and for a stipulated period of minutes) until one, returned to his office after a family lunch for an hour or more, and then had his automobile ride. Later, at the behest of Admiral Cary Grayson, his devoted doctor to the end of his life, he took up golf.

House continued to live primarily in his apartment in New York, where Wilson stayed on his visits there, even sharing a bathroom with his host, but the Colonel's visits to the capital were frequent, and he always stayed at the White House. House was absolutely sincere in his belief that Wilson was the hope of the civilized world, but he also believed that that hope would only be realized by a Wilson directed and moderated by House.

Indeed, considering the outward attitude of consistent admiration, of almost hero worship that House maintained toward the president, his private conclusions about Wilson's failings are sufficiently startling. One must remember that they are without spite; it was his simple duty, as he probably saw it, to be constantly assessing the assets and liabilities of the man who was to save the world. Here are a few:

He dodges trouble. Let me put something up to him that is disagreeable, and I have great difficulty getting him to meet it.

Another phase of his character is the intensity of his prejudices against people. He likes a few and is very loyal to them, but his prejudices are many and often unjust. He finds great difficulty in conferring with men against whom, for some reason, he has a prejudice and in whom he can find nothing good.

I am afraid that the President's characterization of himself as a man with a one-track mind is all too true, for he does not seem to carry along more than one idea at a time.

The President, as I have often said before, is too casual and does the most important things sometimes without much reflection.

We do not know what Wilson really thought of House except in the warmth of his personal letters to him, but he did admit to his second wife, Edith, when she opened her campaign against his friend for lacking a "strong character," that she was right in thinking that intellectually House was not a "great man," that his mind was not "of the first class." But he went on to insist that House provided him with "prudent and far seeing counsel" and that he had "a noble and lovely character." He ended by assuring her: "You are going to love House some day—if only because he loves me and would, I believe, give his life for me."

How little he knew about jealousy, at least in others! That was precisely the reason that she hated his friend.

*   *   *

Tariff reform was one of the big successes of Wilson's first term. It was widely believed that the trusts had used high tariffs, with all their preferential rates and complex shelters, to establish control of the economic system. The administration's proposed bill of reduction of rates, including the virtual elimination of any on wool and sugar, and providing a progressive income tax to make up for the anticipated loss of revenue, produced such an invasion of lobbyists in the capital that Wilson observed "a brick couldn't be thrown without hitting one of them." His public denunciation of the practice was followed by a Senate investigation which revealed for the first time what a gigantic business it had become, and contributed, along with the substantial Democratic majorities in both houses, to the passage of the tariff bill. The effect of the bill, however, was largely nullified by the war, and a Republican Congress in 1922 restored many of the rates.

Wilson acknowledged his debt to House in this matter with the peculiar depth of feeling that always marked his correspondence with his adviser:

> Your letter on the passage of the Tariff Bill gave me the kind of pleasure that seldom comes to a man, and goes so deep that no words are adequate to express it. I think you must know without my putting it into words (for I cannot) how deep such friendship and support goes with me and how large a part it constitutes of such strength as I have in public affairs.

The next great success was the Federal Reserve Act, establishing a reserve system of twelve regional Federal Reserve banks, to be located in various parts of the United States, under the control of a central Federal Reserve Board to be made up of the secretary of the treasury, the comptroller of the currency, and other members to be appointed by the president. The principal idea was to establish regional banks in which the individual commercial banks could safely keep their reserves and to provide a currency that would expand and contract with the demands of the money market.

The previous banknote currency, with government bonds as security, was related only to the amount of bonds available at a particular time and not to the ups and downs of trade. The result was a constant round of desperate money needs and financial panics. Under the proposed legislation the reserve banks could issue currency against commercial assets. Senator Carter Glass of Virginia gave valuable assistance to the president in drafting the act, but almost a year was consumed in congressional wrangling over some of its features, particularly in the composition of its directing board. Wall Street wanted its representatives to dominate it, and the liberals cried "Monopoly!" Wilson wanted it to be made up entirely of government appointees, and the right wing cried "Socialism!" In the end Wilson prevailed, and the great Federal Reserve System was established and has extended its beneficent influence to our own day.

It neither abolished poverty nor redistributed wealth, as

extremists hoped or feared. It simply took away Wall Street's monopoly of credit and provided us with an elastic currency.

Some later commentators have shown disappointment that Wilson was so long in endorsing a child labor law to prohibit the shipping in interstate commerce of goods manufactured in whole or in part by children under the age of fourteen. Such observers live in our age, when the reach of the Commerce Clause has been extended to permit the federal government to do almost anything. In Wilson's day this process had just begun, and even many liberals were dubious about using the clause in what struck them as a deviously indirect way, even to accomplish a humanitarian objective. They still thought child labor was the concern of the states.

After two years in office Wilson had to face the fact, as most if not all presidents must, that if he had satisfied some of his constituents, he had probably displeased quite as many, and for what? He had worked himself to the bone. He told one journalist that he had thought of hanging a sign outside his office reading: "Don't shoot; he's doing his damnedest." And he confessed to a friend that he had urges to buy a false beard and flee the White House to be a free citizen again and have a jolly time. Happily, he always had the consolation of his strong faith, his belief that he was doing the right thing, and the total devotion of his family.

Businessmen complained that he was destroying private enterprise; the rich resented the new income tax on large incomes; capitalists asserted that the Federal Reserve Act had frightened venture capital; legislators shrieked at his dictatorial trespass on legislative functions; ardent reformers were disgruntled that his achievements had fallen so short of their goals. And finally, the Washington storekeepers still resented the losses they had incurred by the simplicity of his inauguration. But as Arthur Walworth has said in his *Woodrow Wilson, American Prophet:* "Within the short space of ten months his administration had gone far in writing into statute the grass roots tide of protest that had carried him into the presidency. The stirrings of unrest that had agitated both political parties had at last been codified under the Constitution by a leader who was sentient, inspiring and wise."

5

THROUGHOUT WILSON'S TWO TERMS, but particularly in the first, Mexican civil wars provided a constant headache. In 1913 General Victoriano Huerta effected a coup d'état in Mexico City and demanded that his government be recognized by the United States and the European powers. Many of the latter, including Great Britain, which had large business interests in the country, thought that, however bad, Huerta's gang might be the best they could hope for. Wilson hesitated; to him Huerta's was a "government of butchers." But he finally accorded it a temporary de facto recognition.

Wilson probably handled a messy situation as well as could be expected, but it has often been said that he allowed his moral disapproval of Huerta to count too much in his decisions. After all, Venustiano Carranza, who now mounted a rebellion against Huerta under the banner of the "Constitutionalists," and Francisco "Pancho" Villa, who led a fight against both, were not much better. Villa, in fact, was worse.

Wilson distrusted his ambassador in Mexico City, Henry Lane Wilson, who was so pro-Huerta that he was supposed to have had a hand in the coup d'état, and sent his friend

William Bayard Hale to investigate matters there. When Hale reported that near chaos existed under the Huerta regime, Wilson recalled his ambassador and appointed, at Bryan's request, former governor John Lind of Minnesota as his successor. In this Wilson suffered from the ill effects of the spoils system so necessary to his good relations with Congress. Lind, who spoke no Spanish and knew nothing about Mexico, was a typical Bryan diplomatic appointment and made a hash of the job. Wilson, indignant at Britain's continued support of Huerta, wanted to invoke the Monroe Doctrine in opposition, but was dissuaded by John Bassett Moore, the State Department's counsel, who pointed out that the doctrine had no relation to the recognition of governments. He then merely requested British assistance in persuading Huerta to retire. Huerta, unsurprisingly, chose not to.

All of Wilson's efforts to bring the Huerta government to an accord with the Constitutionalists having failed, civil war raged, and Huerta was able to establish an iron dictatorship in the areas he controlled. Wilson now openly sided with the Carranza rebels and lifted the arms embargo. It was his hope that, true to their name, they would, with victory, establish constitutional government throughout the land.

His switch was not popular in Britain. As one London editorial put it: "No state pretending to civilization has ever before announced its readiness to supply the anarchical elements in a neighboring community with the means of rapine and massacre for mere profit."

To call the Constitutionalists anarchists may be strong, but it is certainly true that Carranza did not relish advice from Wilson, and that he appalled the peace-seeking president with his stubborn refusal to treat with, and his savage determination to annihilate, his foe.

In 1914 Wilson was faced with the Veracruz crisis. The paymaster of the USS *Dolphin* landed at Tampico without a permit and was arrested by Huerta militia. He was duly returned to his ship, but Admiral Henry T. Mayo intemperately demanded an abject apology. Not only should a twenty-one-gun salute be rendered, but the American flag should be hoisted in a prominent position on shore. Wilson himself took part in the ridiculous negotiations that followed, and when an accord could not be reached, he asked Congress for authority to enforce the admiral's demands and received it by a vote of 337 to 37. He then ordered the occupation of Veracruz, which was accomplished only at the cost of 126 Mexican lives and 19 American.

Reaction throughout the world and particularly in Latin America was harsh, and Wilson's reputation as a statesman suffered badly. Even Carranza disapproved and urged the rapid evacuation of Veracruz. The matter was settled through the mediation of Argentina, Brazil, and Chile at a meeting at Niagara Falls, and the American forces abandoned the occupied city. Huerta shortly thereafter fled to Spain, and Carranza was briefly victorious, until his rule was challenged in the north by the bloody Villa. The latter's massacre of seventeen Americans taken off a Mexican train and his raid over the border into Columbus, New Mexico,

necessitated the dispatch of the punitive expedition of
General John J. Pershing, which embroiled American troops
with Carranza's forces as well as Villa's. A final accord was
not reached until 1917, with Pershing's army withdrawn,
Carranza in essential but precarious control of Mexico, and
Villa still ominously at large. Feelings between Mexico City
and Washington were still decidedly cool, and Mexico remained resolutely neutral throughout World War I.

The nineteen dead Americans at Veracruz remained on
Wilson's conscience. That these men should have paid with
their lives for a trivial dispute over the form of an apology
for an act which had caused no physical hurt or even any
serious inconvenience brought on something of an emotional crisis in the remorseful president, a foreshadowing of
the even greater agony that he was to endure in making the
terrible decisions which the European war would bring.

However, the greatest blow of Wilson's first term was
the death of his wife Ellen, of nephritis leading to kidney
failure, in August of 1914, on almost the very day that war
broke out in Europe. Wilson was shattered. When Dr.
Grayson pronounced her dead, Wilson walked to the window of her room and, looking out, murmured: "Oh, my
God, what am I to do?" Even three months later he told
House that he was broken in spirit and not fit to be president because "he did not think straight any longer and had
no heart for the things he was doing." But he also wrote: "I
do not see the light yet; but it is not necessary for me to see
it: I know that it shines, and I know *where* it shines. . . ."

Yet less than a year later, in the spring of 1915, he was

passionately in love again. Wilson simply could not live without the love and approval of an attractive and sympathetic woman, and when his cousin, Helen Woodrow Bones, who was standing in as a substitute first lady at the White House, introduced him to her friend Edith Bolling Galt, he was immediately smitten. She was the charming forty-two-year-old widow of Norman Galt, a Washington jeweler who had left her, if childless, the prosperous owner of an attractive house where she entertained her select group of friends. The Bollings were an old Virginia family from Wytheville in the western part of the state; Edith even claimed descent from Pocahontas and John Rolfe. She was naturally dazzled by the immediate attentions of the love-struck president and his rapid proposal of marriage, but she was not swept off her feet: she was very much aware of how his public might react to so rapid a recovery from a much touted grief. They would certainly have to wait a full year from Ellen's death, and indeed it was not until December of 1915 that they were wed.

In the meanwhile he wrote to her daily. Here are a few examples of his outpourings:

And, oh, how I needed you tonight, my sweet Edith! What a touch of your hand and a look into your eyes would have meant to me of strength and steadfastness as I made the final decision as to what I should say to Germany.

It may be that if the knight were younger and had beauty of person that matched his love and courage, you would save him the agony of the siege and come out with shining eyes to deliver him the keys with your own hands.

I was interested to meet Mr. Churchill [the American novelist] and found him interesting in some respects, but a subtle comparison always comes up in my mind when I meet men, to a very wonderful person whom I love, and the rest of humanity seems commonplace.

You are my perfect playmate, with whom everything that is gay and mirthful and imaginative in me is at its best.

When bedtime comes and you are not here to crown the day with your sweet sympathy and tenderness and comprehension of my need, how I get by these crises I do not know—how often, how long I shall be able to get by them I dare not try to think or reckon.

He was touched when she was frightened that if he saw the German ambassador, Count Johann von Bernsdorff, alone, some violence might be done to his person! No wonder House observed testily in his journal: "It seems the President is wholly absorbed in this love affair and is neglecting practically everything else."

It became obvious to the presidential circle that he had better get married as soon as possible, but some were apprehensive about how the voters would react to a ceremony where, in the words of the Prince of Denmark, "the funeral baked meats would scantly furnish forth the marriage feast." What about the all-important presidential election of 1916?

McAdoo was apparently one of these, and to him has been attributed the horrid plot that was devised to induce Wilson to postpone his wedding plans. Wilson had loaned to the ever impecunious Mary Peck, who had resumed her Hulbert name, the sum of $7,500 (he was always an extraordinarily generous man for one of a large family and limited means), and this became known. McAdoo, concerned with what political opponents might make of this, in combination with Mrs. Galt, decided that the first thing to do was to eliminate Mrs. Hulbert from his father-in-law's life and correspondence. According to some sources, he claimed to have received an anonymous letter informing him that Mary Hulbert was negotiating the sale of Wilson's letters to her. This, incidentally, was completely untrue; she never even contemplated so low a deed. But Wilson did not take it at all as McAdoo had presumably intended him to. He decided that if his friendship with Mary Hulbert was going to be made public, he had better make a full disclosure of it to Edith.

Edith's response was immediate: "I will stand by you—not for duty—not for pity . . . but for love."

On December 18, 1915, they were married.

"My wife is dead; long live my wife," sneered Theodore Roosevelt. But he too had been a grief-stricken widower who had found a second love in a second marriage. He had waited a bit longer; that was all. Henry Cabot Lodge, who had just lost his own wife, was also critical, but then Wilson could never do anything of which *he* approved.

6

WILSON'S ROLE AS PRESIDENT from July of 1914, when the great war started in Europe, to April of 1917, when he asked Congress for a declaration of war, has been compared, favorably and unfavorably, to Franklin D. Roosevelt's role in the same office from September of 1939, when Hitler invaded Poland, to December of 1941, when Japan attacked Pearl Harbor. Of course, the vital difference was that FDR was working as hard as he could, directly and indirectly, to aid the Allies in every way possible, and even to join them in war if that became necessary, while Wilson, with passionate sincerity, was trying to keep the nation neutral, and aiding the Allies only to the extent that neutrality was not threatened.

As the issues at stake in World War II were and have remained black and white to most Americans (Hitler, Mussolini, and Hirohito were and are still considered so many devils), and as a resounding victory was followed by a nonvindictive peace and the establishment of the United Nations, FDR's prewar policy has been generally approved. Wilson's reluctance to enter the conflict, on the other hand, has been viewed by many as stretching out Armageddon to a point where the wholesale destruction of life made any but a vindictive peace impossible to attain, and that peace ensured another war.

But a change of points of view about the issues at stake in the first war makes Wilson's attitude more sympathetic to us. Having lived through the years of Hitler's holocaust, we are no longer inclined, like our forebears, to buy toilet paper stamped with the Kaiser's image. We have learned that many of the tales of German atrocities in Belgium were invented by British propagandists. Imperial Germany, bad as it was, seems almost gentle seen through the smoke of the gas chambers at Auschwitz. And wasn't there some truth in the argument that the imperialist powers of France and Great Britain saw a rising Germany as a threat to their world domination and wanted to crush it once and for all?

We look back with horror and incredulity on four years of trench warfare in which the Allied and German commanders remorselessly and habitually fed a whole generation of their finest young men into a slaughter bath to gain a few yards of mud and barbed wire. Have England and France ever really recovered from it? What was their victory worth when they had been bled white?

Yet that war engaged the home front in a frenzy of patriotism and hate never seen before. Even when Lloyd George was reluctant to send the huge reinforcements demanded by his ruthless and insatiable generals at the front, wondering if Britain could afford to lose so many, he was still opposed to a negotiated peace. Vera Brittain, in her wonderfully eloquent *Testament of Youth*, tells of men on leave from battle who simply could not communicate with their friends and families at home who persisted in seeing the war as a glorious crusade for civilization in which it should be a privilege to participate, even to die. And when Siegfried Sassoon, who had to be listened to because of his many awards for valor, pleaded with Parliament to put an end to the slaughter and refused to return to the trenches, he was confined to a psychiatric ward.

Years after the armistice, when Lord Oxford, formerly Mr. H. H. Asquith, the first wartime prime minister, was interviewed by an American correspondent, he reacted in this fashion to a question about American peace efforts:

> I asked him if the statesmen of Europe struggling for breath and life during the World War did not ultimately tire of Colonel House and his various peace plans, and ask themselves why this small unofficial person should keep thrusting himself into their affairs. At this Asquith struck the terrace with his cane and said there would have been more of breath and life if the plans of Colonel House had been acted upon.

It was a violent, an ultimately almost hysterical animosity to Germany and all things German that finally swept America, where Teutonic music was barred and where Theodore Roosevelt, stricken with the news of the death in combat of his aviator son Quentin, was still able resolutely to face the prospect that a protracted war might cost him the lives of all his boys. But in 1914 it was largely confined to the eastern seaboard and the more prosperous Protestant families of Anglo-Saxon descent, where Anglophilia flourished. Wilson had to cope with the reactions of four million

Irish Americans who would bitterly resent the British suppression of dissent in Ireland by the Black and Tans and the execution of Roger Casement, eight million German Americans who refused to condemn their land of origin as barbaric, and unspecified millions of liberals and Jews who had no wish to be on the side of an autocratic and anti-Semitic czarist Russia.

But above all there was a widespread feeling that the war was not our war and that we should keep out of it if we possibly could without loss of our national dignity. Wilson shared this view, though he could be as corny as the worst Fourth of July orator when the occasion seemed to demand it. When he saw our flag, for example, he saw "alternate strips of parchment upon which are written the rights of liberty and justice, and strips of blood spilled to vindicate those rights, and then—in the corner—a prediction of the blue serene into which every nation may swim which stands for these great things."

What he saw in the European conflict, however, was something that Roosevelt, and Page, who became almost a lobbyist for Britain, and Robert Lansing, Bryan's interventionist successor as secretary of state, did not see: that civilization could not afford this kind of new "mechanical slaughter." "Where is any longer the glory commensurate with the sacrifice of the millions of men required by modern warfare to carry and defend Verdun?" Wilson wanted to know.

For him the horror and danger transcended the issues, which was why he exasperated the Allies again and again by refusing to see the war in the purely moral light of right against wrong. If he at times saw the Germans as "blood mad," he also saw their opponents as intractable. He concluded: "It would look as if Europe had finally determined to commit suicide, as Carlyle thought it had at the time of the French Revolution—and the only way we can help is by changing the current of its thought."

House wrote him: ". . . you are the only hope left in this torn and distracted world." And it was House whom he would send forth, a dove from his ark, in quest of peace.

House went on several missions to Europe in search of possibilities of an entente; his third trip, from the end of 1915 through the early months of 1916, was the most important. He had been in correspondence with Sir Edward Grey, the British foreign secretary, and he had received the impression that an American offer to negotiate a peace might not be unwelcome. House visualized secret sessions between the warring powers and a peace devised that would restore Belgium, give France assurances of national security, and set up some sort of international league for the preservation of world amity. The United States would line up against the side that rejected such reasonable terms.

"I feel that you do not need any instructions," Wilson told the departing House. "You exactly echo my own views and purposes." It was just at the time of his second marriage, which may help to explain such preoccupation. House at this point had in his own mind progressed a good deal further than the president in his readiness for war. He had taken in the looming possibility of an Allied defeat and

69

foresaw the unpleasant situation of his militarily unpre-
pared country facing across an Atlantic stripped of the
protection of the British navy a victorious and aggressive German empire bristling with arms. His idea was to
prepare, secretly with the British and French, terms of
peace framed in such a way as to make it probable that
Germany would be the one to reject them, in which event
America would enter the war on the side of the Allies.
House certainly took a lot on himself in his talks with Grey,
but the latter and Lloyd George, now prime minister,
seemed to encourage him, and he crossed to Paris, where his
reception was considerably cooler. In Germany he did not
disclose what he had discussed with the British and engaged in some rather irrelevant talk about freedom of the
seas which he must have known the British would never
agree to.

Returning to London he signed the House-Grey Mem-
orandum to embody their understanding that President
Wilson "was ready, on hearing from France and England
that the moment was opportune, to propose that a conference should be summoned to put an end to the war. Should
the Allies accept this proposal, and should Germany refuse
it, the United States would enter the war against Germany."

Before it was signed Wilson had the word "probably"
inserted before "enter." Obviously, this made the whole
matter a farce, and the British and French governments
promptly rejected the document.

House has been accused of naïveté and overstepping his
authority, but what was his authority? Had not Wilson

given him carte blanche? And so far as naïveté is concerned, perhaps it was naïveté in him to dream that any peace at all was possible. As he wrote Wilson from Paris in February of 1915:

> In each government that I have visited I have found stubbornness, determination, selfishness and cant. One continually hears self-glorification and the highest motives attributed to themselves because of their part in the war. But I may tell you that my observation is that incompetent statesmanship and selfishness is at the bottom of it all. It is not so much a breaking down of civilization as a lack of wisdom in those that govern; and history, I believe, will bring an awful indictment against those who were short-sighted and selfish enough to let such a tragedy happen.

By the end of 1915 the war had taken on the grim and permanent pattern which was to last to the armistice. Germany had declared the waters around Great Britain to be a war zone in which all enemy vessels could be sunk on sight without warning, and the British had responded with a total blockade of the enemy, prohibiting trade not only with Germany but with Belgium and Holland, neighboring non-belligerents. The naval aspect of the conflict, with its attendant threat to neutral shipping, was naturally what most concerned Americans. The army aspect, largely confined to the slaughter in the trenches in Belgium and northern France, appalled our newspaper readers but did not affect our foreign policy. The fortunes of war in this embattled area would favor one side or another from month to month, so that the Allied Powers might be willing to listen to peace overtures one day and the Central Powers the next. But the receptive mood never lasted long enough to bring about even a truce.

In April of 1915 Wilson made a speech in Philadelphia which startled the world and did him great damage in the eyes of the Allies and their American sympathizers. He said:

> The example of America must be the example not merely of peace because it will not fight, but of peace because it is the healing and elevating influence of the world, and strife is not. There is such a thing as a man being too proud to fight. There is such a thing as a nation being so right that it does not need to convince others by force that it is right.

Wilson was dismayed by the indignant and sneering reaction to his use of the term "proud" by those who saw the Allies as engaged in a struggle to save civilization, and he tried to have it eliminated from a printed version of his address, but the damage was done.

House was immune to the growing and passionate faith among the Allies and an increasing number of Americans that the war was a crusade against Satan. He was disgusted with Cecil Spring-Rice, the British ambassador in Washington, who believed, almost hysterically, that House should have no dealings with the German envoy, and he regarded Walter Hines Page, Spring-Rice's opposite number in London, more as an officer of the British Crown than an American diplomat. But House also knew the importance of these diplomats in the war that he now felt we should enter to ensure our national security and obtain a decent peace treaty, and he tried in vain to keep Wilson from antagonizing our future Allies by stating in public what both he and the president privately believed: that "the causes and objects of the war" were "obscure." But Wilson was obdurate and put the offending sentence in his next public appeal for a negotiated peace. House noted bitterly: "He seems obsessed with that thought and he cannot write or talk on the subject of the war without voicing it. It has done more to make him unpopular in the Allied countries than anything he has done, and it will probably keep him from taking the part which he ought to take in peace negotiations. . . . It is all so unnecessary. He could have done and said the same things in a different way."

In the summer of 1916 the war seemed to be going unfavorably for Germany. The French had withstood the terrible onslaught at Verdun; the British were advancing in the Somme, and Romania had entered the war on the Allied side. On the other hand, the submarine warfare was threatening Britain with a loss of imports vital to her very being, and of the five billion pounds that the war cost her daily, two billion had to be found in the United States. Wilson calculated that the time might have come for another bid for peace. And he was not averse to putting economic pressure on the Allies.

House's diary reveals the tumult of his fears and anticipations at this time. He even contemplated the possibility that if the Allies rejected the peace offer and Germany ac-

73

cepted it while at the same time relaxing the fury of her submarine warfare, which was antagonizing more and more Americans, the United States might actually end up on the side of the Central Powers with a navy outgunned by the superior British one! But he would always go along with any endeavor to halt the carnage in Europe.

In December of 1916 German authorities anticipated Wilson by presenting Joseph Grew, the American attaché, with a proposal for peace talks. Wilson indicated approval but called attention to the fact that each side claimed to be fighting "to make the rights of weak peoples and small states as secure against aggression or denial in the future as the rights and privileges of the great and powerful states now at war." He also called for a league of nations.

Secretary of State Lansing was afraid that the president's statement might be interpreted as meaning that the United States was in favor of a German-slanted peace and sought to contradict it in a public announcement that "we were drawing nearer to the verge of war." Wilson was furious and considered asking for his resignation, but decided against it, facing the fact that he had now more and more to deal with belligerent interventionists, even in his immediate circle. We know, for example, that Lansing, though recommended for his post by House, believed that Wilson's judgment was clouded by his inability to accept facts if they conflicted with "his semi-divine power to select the right." This opinion was echoed by Spring-Rice, adored in Washington's intellectual circles and close friends with Roosevelt, Lodge, and Henry Adams, who described the president in a letter to Arthur Balfour as "a mysterious, a rather Olympian personage and shrouded in darkness from which issue occasional thunderbolts." And as for Page, it may suffice to mention that on his death a memorial plaque was unveiled in Westminster Abbey "to the friend of Britain in her direst need," something which, as one historian has observed, should never happen to an ambassador.

Germany, having opened the peace feelers, now drew back. The fortunes of war had turned. Romania had been quickly knocked out, and the British offensive in the Somme had slowed. Germany would state no terms of peace, but simply suggested a meeting of the belligerents at a neutral spot. And discussion of a league of nations could be postponed until the end of hostilities.

And now the Allies at last stated their terms: evacuation by Germany of all territory occupied during the war and full indemnities for all damage incurred. Were they stating impossible conditions to drive Germany into unrestricted submarine warfare and force America into the war? At any rate, Wilson's peace drive collapsed. He would try nothing more until his address to Congress on January 22, 1917, when he called for a "peace without victory," which angered the Allies. He even told Lansing in February of that year that he believed it would be best for the world if the war ended in a draw.

Yet during all his peace efforts German submarine warfare was slowly building up American fury. The British in enforcing their sea blockade of enemy ports angered Americans by blacklisting firms that did any business with Germans or Austrians and by the high-handed way in which they stopped and searched the mail of neutral vessels. But these measures did not cost lives, as did the sinking of Allied or neutral vessels that happened to be carrying American passengers.

The irate feeling aroused by the sinkings seems strange to us who have witnessed the ruthless totality of modern war. After all, Germany was fighting a strangling blockade which sought to starve her people into submission and which was continued in force even after the armistice until a treaty was signed. The only way she could fight it on seas controlled by the British navy was by the submarine. The "cruiser rules" of international law required that a passenger ship must be warned before it was sunk so that those on board might be given a chance to disembark. But if the vessel was armed, as many were, the submarine surfacing to give the warning was an easy target. Such etiquette was reminiscent of the eighteenth-century battle in which a French commander gave an enemy the invitation to fire first.

Bryan, who had resigned as secretary of state in protest of Wilson's stern note to Germany in the *Lusitania* crisis, made the sensible proposal that if we really wanted to stay out of the war, we should forbid our citizens to travel on armed merchantmen of any nationality. Why not? Let them do so at their own risk. But that was not the mood of the nation, and angry notes flew back and forth between Berlin and Washington after the sinkings of enemy and neutral merchantmen and passenger ships, armed and unarmed, with loss of American lives, in a desperate effort to work out some kind of modus vivendi.

The greatest crisis arose in May of 1915 over the sinking in the Irish Sea of the British passenger liner *Lusitania* with the loss of more than a thousand lives, many of them American. The public outrage was great, and Wilson demanded that Germany acknowledge the illegality of the sinking, pay reparations, and agree in the future to abide by the cruiser rules. While the matter was still under negotiation, in March of 1916, an unarmed ferryboat, the *Sussex*, under a French flag, was sunk in the English Channel without warning, injuring but not killing four Americans. At this, perhaps to the general surprise, the Germans offered a pledge, known as the Sussex pledge, to abide in future by the cruiser rules. And for several months they did, which considerably lessened the tension between the two nations.

There had been a sharp division in the German high command between those who advocated a ruthless submarine war to bring Britain to her knees and secure a quick victory before the United States, however outraged, could enter the war, and those who believed that the advantages of such a submarine campaign would not counterbalance the danger of American intervention. The second opinion was the one that temporarily prevailed.

An incident in connection with the stiff *Lusitania* protest sent to Germany is worth relating because of its effect on the all-important feud between the president and Republican senator Henry Cabot Lodge of Massachusetts. At the urging of Bryan (just prior to his resignation) Wilson had written a "tip" or unofficial news release that "administrative circles" did not anticipate that the Germans would be offended by the stiffness of the official note of complaint that had been sent to Berlin. On the advice of some of his cabinet, however, Wilson did not release the tip. Lodge heard and publicized the story slightly differently. His version was that Wilson had written it as a postscript to the official note and quashed it only when certain cabinet members had threatened to resign. Wilson's reply was: "No postscript or amendment to the *Lusitania* note was ever written." When Lodge ultimately learned the full truth of the matter, he was profoundly disgusted at such a quibble over the definition of a tip or a postscript.

The home front also had its troubles. Threatened with a strike of four hundred thousand railroad workers which would have paralyzed industry, Wilson acted promptly and vigorously by inducing Congress to establish the eight-hour day for rail employees, raise rates, and, if necessary, take over the operation of the lines. Wilson's action showed a distinct advance in his constitutional thinking over the time when he had declined to act on child labor.

He also took occasion to make clear that his peace efforts were not inspired by any particular sympathy for imperial Germany. To the head of a pro-German, anti-British propaganda organization he sent this open letter: "I would feel deeply mortified to have you or anyone like you vote for me. Since you have access to many disloyal Americans and I have not, I will ask you to convey this message to them."

The mood of the country, particularly in view of the temporary lull in illegal sinkings, was still for peace, and the Democratic Convention of 1916 in St. Louis was quick to nominate "the man who has kept us out of war." The occasion was marked with fervent oratory; that of Senator Ollie M. James of Kentucky, the chairman, was particularly florid: "When the last great day shall come, and before the Court of God the nations of this earth shall march in judgment review, . . . I can see our President holding in his hand the accusing picture . . . of Christ upon the battlefield, with the dead and dying all around him . . . and above his head written these words: 'And He said unto them: love one another.' When that day shall come, who is it that would have our President exchange places with the blood-spattered monarchs of the Old World?"

The Republicans in Chicago chose former Supreme Court justice Charles Evans Hughes to run against Wilson. Roosevelt, a strong interventionist on the war issue, and who regarded Hughes with some skepticism as wobbly on preparedness, was nonetheless so anti-Wilson, whose diplomacy vis-à-vis Germany he had characterized with the phrase "shaking first his fist and then his finger," that he swung his Progressives, so far as he could, back into the Republican ranks.

It looked for a time as if Hughes might win the election. He had the backing of Roosevelt and many of those who believed that we should enter the war on the side of the Allies or at least do more to bolster their cause. He had the support of some of the great financial leaders who had been

shocked by what they regarded as Wilson's prolabor attitude in bringing about a settlement of the threatened national railroad strike. There were those who felt that Wilson
had mishandled the Mexican civil war; there were those
who found his personality cold and forbidding, and those
who felt that a successful lawyer and former Supreme
Court justice was a preferable intellectual to a college professor. But the slogan "He kept us out of war" counterbal-
anced all.

Wilson himself sided with the pessimists, and to avoid a
lame-duck presidency (which at that time would have
lasted four months) in a period of international crisis, he
adopted a secret plan suggested by House by which it was
agreed that if the vote went to Hughes, Vice President
Marshall and Secretary of State Lansing would resign their
offices, whereupon Wilson would appoint Hughes as Lansing's successor and himself resign the presidency.

Hughes, however, did not win, though he awakened one
morning to be told that he had. The final count against him
was narrow but decisive. The enthusiasts for peace, on the
other hand, had little cause to rejoice. The publication of
the telegram of Arthur Zimmerman, German foreign secretary, to his ambassador in Mexico, offering that nation its
former territories in Texas, New Mexico, and Arizona if it
would join with Germany in the event of war with the
United States, intercepted by the British and promptly (one
can be sure!) forwarded to Washington, created a national
furor.

On January 31, 1917, the submarine party in Germany

triumphed with the announcement that, after a brief grace period for neutral shipping, *all* ships in a broad zone around Britain and France and in the Mediterranean around Italy would be sunk without warning. The sole concession was that one American passenger ship, plainly marked, would be allowed a weekly passage between Falmouth and New York!

By March 20 three American vessels had been sunk, and Wilson summoned his cabinet to ask them if he should call Congress into extraordinary session, and if so, what he should put before them. Lansing has described him as "smiling as genially and composedly as if nothing of importance was to be considered." Yet this had a "sobering effect" on the silent group. The vote was unanimous that Congress should be summoned and asked for a declaration of war, which on April 6 was given.

7

THERE WERE THOSE who wondered if a president who had tried so stubbornly and (in some views) so almost cringingly to preserve diplomatic relations with the increasingly arrogant and ruthless Hohenzollern monarchy would be able to wage an effective war. They remembered with scorn his "too proud to fight" speech and his consistent reluctance in any public utterance to credit the Allies with fighting what increasing numbers believed to be a crusade that might ultimately save America from invasion and possible defeat. Roosevelt's intemperate reaction was that Wilson was a demagogue "without a touch of the heroic in his cold, selfish and timid soul."

Even House had his doubts, though he did all he could to back up his chief in a moment of understandable depression. The situation on the eve of war had driven Wilson's friend from his usual caution and flattery, and for once he had spoken out boldly:

> I told him a crisis had come in his administration different from anything he had yet encountered, and I was anxious that he should meet it in a creditable way so that this influence would not be lessened when he came to do the great work which should necessarily follow

the war. I said it was not as difficult a situation as many he had successfully met, but that it was one for which he was not well fitted. He admitted this and said he did not believe he was fitted for the presidency under such conditions. I thought he was too refined, too civilized, too intellectual, too cultivated, not to see the incongruity and absurdity of war. It needs a man of coarser fibre and one less a philosopher than the President to conduct a brutal, vigorous and successful war.

This might seem hardly the kind of fight talk a beleaguered chief of state needed, but House knew his man if the following entry is to be credited:

I made him feel, as Mrs. Wilson told me later, that he was not up against so difficult a situation as he had imagined. In my argument I said that everything that he had to meet in this emergency had been thought out time and again in other countries, and all we had to do was to take experience as our guide and not worry over the manner of doing it.

If Mrs. Wilson really approved of House's bizarre method of bracing her husband's morale, it must have been effective, for she was to prove the Colonel's most implacable enemy. She was now not only the president's wife but his daily and at times almost hourly companion, the sharer of all his thoughts and emotions. She did not seek to dominate her husband or even to contribute to his store of ideas. She worshiped him as the great man of his era and saw her role as one of constant and unquestioning support, a kind of priestess at the altar of a deity. Unfortunately, she was extremely jealous of this prerogative and became the bitter enemy of any other whom she suspected of seeking to share her role. She also did not hesitate to put her husband's personal welfare above any other consideration of man or state.

The fears about Wilson's wartime leadership proved groundless. As the historian Thomas A. Bailey has said, it was one of the ironies of history that the peace-loving Wilson "obtained greater success in making war than in making peace."

All was now cold efficiency. A "War Cabinet" was established of central committees whose chairmen met every Wednesday with the president and the secretaries of the navy, the treasury, and war: the Committee on Public Information, headed by George Creel; the War Industries Board, by Bernard Baruch; the Food Administration, by Herbert Hoover; the Fuel Administration, by Harry Garfield, son of the late president; the Shipping Board, by Edward Hurley; and the War Trade Board, by Vance McCormick.

When Theodore Roosevelt, aged fifty-nine, almost blind in one eye and still suffering from the effects of a near fatal exploratory expedition on the River of Doubt in Brazil, but as indomitable as ever, came himself to the White House to request permission to organize a division under his command to be sent immediately to the western front, he was at first coolly and later more warmly received by the president, but his project was not approved. It was a planned, mechanical war, and it would not be won by dramatic and heroic gestures. The many friends of TR were offended, but the military endorsed Wilson.

The immense job of girding America for the conflict, of producing the ships and armaments to send and equip more than a million men to fight in France, showed Wilson at his most dedicated and best. The Allies were exhausted and perilously close to defeat. Britain's sea losses to submarines threatened her ability to sustain the fight, and French morale at the front was ominously low. The military leaders of both countries assumed that with their long experience in battle, they could treat the green American troops as mere supplementary forces, to be mixed with theirs and under their orders, and that American industry would be more or less harnessed to meet their demands. But Wilson made it very clear that the United States was an associate rather than an ally and would retain its independence in organizing its war effort and even in the deployment of its armed forces.

It was fortunate that he did so, for new thinking was badly needed at this point in the seemingly endless war. Wilson and Admiral William S. Sims brought new solutions to the submarine problem and worked out a convoy system, manned with American destroyers which operated in British waters under British command, so effective that by the time American troops were arriving in Europe at the rate of ten thousand a day, the menace had been almost eliminated. A draft was needed, and Wilson obtained a Selective Service Act from Congress, and the vast American army so recruited, when sent to the front under General Pershing, fought as a national unit and not as an adjunct to the forces already there.

While the Americans were gaining victories at Château-Thierry and Belleau Wood and the Allies were advancing in the Somme area, and the Germans were at last losing their initiative, Wilson was not neglecting plans for the peace that was now beginning to loom. Colonel House and a brilliant team of international scholars, including Walter Lippmann, operating under the name of "The Inquiry," were meeting secretly in New York to gather a vast body of information about Europe to assist the American representatives to any future peace discussions. Harold Nicolson, a British diplomat at the Paris Conference, was to say of this group: "Had the Treaty of Paris been drafted solely by the American experts, it would have been one of the wisest as well as the most scientific document ever devised." A principal product of The Inquiry, the final draft of which would be hammered out by Wilson and House working alone together, was the famous "Fourteen Points," to constitute the basis of any peace.

The first six points were general; they called for open covenants of peace, openly arrived at; freedom of the seas; removal of economic frontiers; reduction of armaments; and settlement of colonial claims. The others were specific, calling for evacuation of territory occupied by the Germans in Russia, Belgium, and elsewhere; ceding of Alsace-Lorraine to France; reallocation of borders in the Austro-Hungarian Empire, Italy, and the Balkans, with due weight given to the self-determination of peoples; and the dismantlement of Turkey. It was in reliance on the Fourteen Points, and the more favorable treatment of the defeated nations, that Germany, in bitter disillusionment, would later claim that she had signed the armistice in November of 1918.

If Wilson gained one victory in that month, he lost another. The congressional elections of that year, despite his ill-advised plea to the nation that a Republican victory would be interpreted by European chiefs as a repudiation of his leadership, resulted in a majority for his political opponents in both houses and the appointment of Henry Cabot Lodge as chairman of the Foreign Affairs Committee.

The handwriting was thus splashed on the wall, and in great capital letters, that any treaty agreed upon by the peace conference to be assembled in Paris would have to be ratified by a Senate controlled by a party disposed to be severely critical of the president. Had Wilson himself not pointed to the danger, as far back as 1885, that the federal system might one day be seriously unbalanced by "an irresponsible exertion" of the Senate's "semi-executive powers in regard to the foreign policy of the government"? Well, that day was at hand.

I think most historians today agree that Wilson should not have gone to Paris. He should have stayed in Washington, remote from the bickerings of the vindictive victors, with a voice all the more powerful for not being drowned in angry debate and an opportunity to review in quiet isolation each new proposition and compromise submitted. It would also have provided him with the chance to confer with Republican leaders and keep them up-to-date on the process of the Parisian talks. It was Congress, after all, that was going to decide the issue that Wilson most cared about: whether we should join any league of nations growing out of the peace conference. House so advised him. Many so advised him. No president, it was pointed out, had ever before left the United States while in office, not even the peripatetic Roosevelt. But no, he *would* go and bring peace, a just peace, to all peoples.

Roosevelt issued a rough statement to newsmen that Wilson no longer represented the United States. "Our allies and our enemies and Mr. Wilson himself should all understand that Mr. Wilson has no authority whatsoever to speak for the American people at this time. His leadership has just been emphatically repudiated by them. The newly elected Congress comes far nearer than Mr. Wilson to having the right to speak the purposes of the American people at this moment. Mr. Wilson and his fourteen points . . . have ceased to have any shadow of right to be accepted as expressive of the will of the American people."

Worse still was the appointment of the four peace commissioners to accompany the president. The choice of Lansing, as secretary of state, was indicated, and that of General Tasker Bliss, as a military representative, was perhaps also called for; but for House, as we have seen, this was a nomination that destroyed his essential value to the president as an alter ego who had no existence or ambition but to assist Wilson with his inner debates and hard decisions. House, now clothed with independent authority, had a duty to act as House as well as Wilson's House, and there would be a conflict. Why then did he take the post? Because the making of world peace and the creation of world government had been the dream of his whole life and took precedence at last over the submergence of his personality in that of his chief.

Which left just one position for a Republican, though why just one, we do not know. Surely the president could have taken any number that he wished. Anyway, had that one been a prominent party member such as Elihu Root or ex-president Taft or even Lodge himself, it might have satisfied the opposition in Congress. But Wilson chose Henry White, a distinguished and respected diplomat, a former ambassador to Italy and France, a rich, affable, and socially charming gentlemen, and a Republican, of course, but one who had never run for elective office and whose contributions to the party, if any, had been purely financial. As Lodge snarled, the president had appointed four Wilsons and Henry White!

Nobody, anyway, knew better than White what a mistake his appointment had been—a virtual insult to the party in whose inner councils he had played no part. Why then did he accept? Because, it has been said, he was afraid Wilson might make an even worse choice and antagonize the Republicans further. He was a patriotic and conscientious man and wanted a workable peace to come out of the Paris talks. He hoped that he might play a useful role by keeping in touch with his good friend Lodge and briefing him by letter on what was going on. Might this not ameliorate the senator's wrath at being excluded? Here is an example of how in March of 1919 White tried to sell a league of nations to his recalcitrant friend:

> In view of the fact that more than seven million, two hundred and forty-odd thousand men have been killed in this war, that five million more men have been entirely incapacitated for any sort of usefulness during the rest of their lives, either by blindness or the loss of both arms or legs or one of the innumerable reasons which you can imagine, I cannot but feel that a strenuous effort must be made to try to prevent a return to the barbarous methods hitherto prevailing, which will, of course, be even more barbarous hereafter in view of the constant scientific improvements in weapons for the destruction of human life.

But his appeal fell on deaf ears.

It has been widely and truly observed that the tremendous, the earthshaking welcome that the American president received from packed crowds in London, Paris, and Rome was the last thing that a man of his temperament needed before sitting down to deal with bargainers as wily, determined, and vindictive as Lloyd George, Clemenceau, and Orlando. For Wilson's worst political fault lay in his faith that he had, more than other leaders, a sense of the will of the common people, and that he was divinely ordained to carry it out. Again and again in his careers, both academic and political, he tended to appeal any adverse decision to the review of some larger body, and the ringing shouts in the streets and squares of the Old World must have made him feel like a messiah endowed with the vision to understand that the multitude was on the side of the merciful angels of a fair and lasting peace and that only a minority of stubborn old men wanted to crush the enemy to dust. He never learned that the only leader who can take political advantage of the momentary enthusiasm of the common man is a dictator who can use its force to blast his way to power; a democrat must abide by the decision of those whom the common man has elected to represent him. In our own day we have seen a president undergo the humiliation of an impeachment process despite the fact that a majority of the voters clearly disapproved.

Wilson wanted fair treatment for all, including the enemy, but above all, far above all, he wanted a league of nations to prevent future wars. He had worked out the basic plan: there would be a general assembly representing all nations, but only the bigger ones would have permanent seats. There would be a secretariat in Geneva and an international court. And the crux of it all was contained in the proposed Article 10 of the Covenant of the League, which committed the signers "to respect and preserve as against external aggression the territorial integrity and existing political independence of the States members of the League. In case of any such aggression the Executive Council shall advise upon the means by which this obligation shall be fulfilled."

The cordiality of the opening days of the Paris talks did not last for long. The acrimonious demands of the victor nations were soon in conflict with Wilson's freely expressed idealism, his insistence that the nations were faced with the challenge to make a just peace without precedent in the dark annals of history. It would be shameful, he argued, if the strong simply divided up the weak and then formed a league to safeguard the dirty work. When it was pointed out to him that such had been the way with peace conferences in the past, he expressed the hope that "even by reference" the 1815 Treaty of Vienna should not again be brought into the proceedings. The press both in Paris and London became critical of Wilson, and Lord Curzon, the British ambassador to France, reported that the delays in the peace conference were entirely to be laid at the door of the American president.

The time would come when Clemenceau would actually denounce Wilson as pro-German! "In that event," Wilson retorted, "do you wish me to return home?" "I do not wish you to go home," Clemenceau replied, "but I intend to do so myself." And he left the chamber.

But what all parties soon learned was that the American president wanted his league so badly that he could be made to pay almost any price for it. In the play *In Time to Come* by Howard Koch, the scene of an imaginary interview between Wilson and Lodge in the White House, after the former's return to Washington, has Lodge retorting to the president: "You've got the world saddled with a treaty you despise for the sake of a covenant nobody else really wants." There was much truth in it.

Harold Nicolson in *Peacemaking, 1919* explains Wilson's compromises as follows:

> It is not a sufficient explanation to contend that President Wilson was conceited, obstinate, nonconformist and reserved. He was also a man obsessed, possessed. He believed, as did Marat, that he was the physical embodiment of "la volonte generale." He was obsessed by the conviction that the League covenant was his own revelation and the solution of all human difficulties. He was profoundly convinced that if his new Charter of the Rights of Nations could be framed and included in the Peace Treaties it mattered little what inconsistencies, what injustice, what flagrant violations of his own principles, those treaties might contain.

John Maynard Keynes echoes Nicolson in his essay "The Council of Four," in which he maintains that Wilson was the victim of his theological and Presbyterian temperament. He could allow no abatement of the verbal inspiration of the Fourteen Points, which therefore became, for his wily opponents, a "document for gloss and interpretation and for all the intellectual apparatus of self-deception." Wilson, by insisting that Lloyd George and Clemenceau should show him that what they wanted fell within the words of the pronouncements that were binding on him, gave rise to "the weaving of that web of sophistry and Jesuitical exegesis that was finally to clothe with insincerity the language and substance of the whole Treaty."

And Winston Churchill in *The Crisis* suggests what might have been the alternative. "If President Wilson had set himself from the beginning to make common cause with Lloyd George and Clemenceau, the whole force of these three great men, the heads of the dominant nations, might have played with plenary and beneficent power over the whole scene of European tragedy. He consumed his own strength and theirs in conflict in which he was always worsted."

What was left of the Fourteen Points in the end? Very little. Covenants were not openly arrived at; the freedom of the seas was not even mentioned; free trade and disarmament (except in the case of the enemy) were ignored; the German colonies were divided up among the victors. More specifically, the Saar Valley was ceded to France for fifteen years; the province of Shandong in China went to Japan; the South Tirol and Fiume were given to Italy; and despite the affirmation of self-determination of peoples, a Polish Corridor was stretched across Teutonic territory to the Baltic. Worst of all, Germany was crippled with reparations impossible to pay, including pensions for Allied servicemen, and made to sign a humiliating and pointless war-guilt clause.

It might be noted here that the principle of self-determination is as difficult to apply in our day as it was in Wilson's. Will it stop short of splitting our planet into an impossible number of small, bickering nations? It may be well to remember of our two most revered presidents that Washington fought a war to affirm the doctrine, and Lincoln one to deny it.

Early in 1919 the president returned briefly to Washington. House, who understood that his chief's principles were being seriously undermined in the negotiations but who believed that such compromises were necessary to produce a treaty, took the occasion, in bidding him farewell, to remind him that one of Wilson's most admired statesmen, Edmund Burke, had said that "to govern is to compromise." But Wilson had replied grimly: "I do not agree with you or with Burke. I have found that you get nothing in this world without fighting for it."

This may have foreshadowed the break with House. When Wilson returned to Paris and reviewed what his friend had done in his absence, he exclaimed bitterly to Edith: "House has given away everything I had won before we left Paris." Rejoining the conference, he stiffened his positions, creating a stalemate in negotiations until April 1919, when he was felled by a serious illness. At the time it was thought to be the terrible influenza that was killing almost as many people as the war, but Dr. Weinstein believes it was another stroke.

Wilson's behavior on recovery was marked by several eccentricities. He was afraid that the servants in the Hotel Murat, the great palace assigned to him, were all French spies; he was apprehensive about robbers; he tried to rearrange the furniture in his study, even pushing chairs around the room himself; he became fussy about details of household maintenance; and, while he should have been concerning himself with the peace of the world, he would irritably scold the staff for improper use of the automobiles!

Heckscher has written of him in these days: "He was a man in haste, insisting on getting things done, often without regard for the niceties of principle and logic that had earlier characterized his approach. Had he not fallen ill, Wilson would undoubtedly have brought matters to a head by some drastic and dramatic move. But it was now as if he saw everything in a terrifying perspective. Sickness had sharpened his resolve, giving him a sense of passing time and of his own mortality."

Things, he may have decided, had gone on long enough! He had to get on with the job; he had to bring home a treaty, as soon as possible, and to do this he had to compromise. At nine-thirty on the evening of the very day the treaty was at last signed, Wilson boarded the train for the first leg of his journey home. House was there to bid him good-bye. The two men were never to meet again.

8

———

THE YOUNG HENRY CABOT LODGE, teaching American colonial history at Harvard in the 1870s, was shocked to read in the paper of one of his students, Edward Channing, that Francis Higginson, famed preacher of seventeenth-century Salem, was a "hypocrite."

"Mr. Channing," he demanded, "do you know that Mr. Higginson was your ancestor?"

"Yes, sir."

"Do you think it well to speak thus of your ancestor?"

Certainly Lodge did not speak ill of his own, who were quite as distinguished as his pupil's. He inherited a fierce pride of origin as well as a considerable fortune made in foreign trade and clipper ships. He believed that the early Puritans had been quite right in seeking their freedom in their own way and "very often quite right in coercing other people."

He would demonstrate the same confidence in himself during his long tenure in Congress, from 1887 to his death in 1924: his first six years in the House, the rest in the Senate.

As Lodge would pit a will as strong as Wilson's against the latter's and reduce to tatters the president's dream of world government, it may be well to consider here certain aspects of his biography.

As the only son of a wealthy and adoring Bostonian widow, he was raised with every supposed advantage, but never lost sight of the obligation of the privileged to set an example to the people. New England to the core, he trained himself for a life of action by studying law and for one of scholarship by earning a doctor's degree in history. Despite the many activities of a full political life, he would write several respectable if little-remembered volumes on American history. He studied German and Italian and learned Anglo-Saxon, and his contribution to *Essays in Anglo-Saxon Law*, studded, according to one learned commentator, "with scholarship in the manner of the most formidable German models," stoutly maintained the theory (since discredited by modern scholars) that the nascent feudalism of the Anglo-Saxons provided the base for the later full-grown system of William the Conqueror and his Norman invaders. It is also interesting to note that as editor of the *International Review*, he published in 1879 the first scholarly article of a young Princeton senior named Woodrow Wilson.

Lodge's lifelong friendship with the Adams brothers, Henry and Brooks, particularly the former, began at an early date, when he took Henry's course in medieval history at Harvard, in which later, as a graduate and teacher, he assisted him. But he was particularly attracted by the brothers' eagerness to establish an independent political party to clean up the fetid sty of corruption that a long Republican rule had made of postbellum Washington. There was a fundamental difference, however, between the Adamses' philosophy and Lodge's. Henry and Brooks saw their role as that of perennial observers and mordant critics; action was to be left to those who did not disdain the grime of politics. Lodge wanted to get into the fray, grime and all. Henry Adams had said that no one should be in politics unless he would rather not be there, but such detachment did not sit well with Lodge's temperament. He loved the whole business from dais to back rooms, which was why he was so good at it.

Henry Adams, in his *Education*, was to put the difference between them this way:

> With Lodge himself, as scholar, fellow instructor, co-editor of the *North American Review*, and political reformer from 1873 to 1878, he had worked intimately, but with him afterwards as politician he had not much relation; and since Lodge had suffered what Adams thought the misfortune of becoming not only a Senator but a Senator from Massachusetts—a singular social relation which Adams had known only as fatal to friends—a superstitious student, intimate with the laws of historical fatality, would rather have recognized him only as an enemy; but apart from this accident he valued Lodge highly, and in the waste places of average humanity had been greatly dependent on his house.

It had not, anyway, taken Lodge long to recognize that an independent progressive party was not the way to get things done in politics. Liberals and idealists, he found, were apt to be too stuck on their own theories, so that they were constantly forming splinter groups and vitiating their own power base. Without in any way diminishing his devotion to and admiration of the Adams brothers, he wedded himself to the Republican Party in the hope that it would clean its own house and beneficently rule the land. And to this faith he remained loyal for life. Vide his ringing dedication of a later date: "To this great Republican organization and the Republican principles, and to nothing else we profess unaltering allegiance, and we find in so doing a greater freedom and more real independence than personal factors in personal politics can ever hope to offer."

But a grim test awaited him. The Republican presidential convention in Chicago of 1884 nominated as its candidate James G. Blaine of Maine, the prime target of every liberal, the very symbol to many of rottenness in the political body. The high-minded Brahmins of Beacon Street and Commonwealth Avenue, the society in which Lodge had been reared and from which he had picked his closest friends, turned up their noses, almost en masse, at the prospect of such a chief of state and deserted their party to earn the celebrated title of "mugwumps." What was Lodge to do?

In the end he stood by the party, he and his new (and soon to be intimate) friend and fellow delegate at the convention, the young Theodore Roosevelt of New York. They had fought together to resist the juggernaut of the "Plumed Knight," but when they failed they had agreed together to stand by the choice of the party. Lodge justified it in this way: "As a delegate I felt in honor bound to do so, because if I had announced that I could not support Blaine, I should never have been chosen a delegate. The pledge was tacit but distinct."

In Boston, and in Nahant, his hometown, few agreed with him. William Everett accused him "not of a change of mind but of a change of soul." In some circles he was virtually ostracized. This caused him a bitterness that long survived the rancor of his friends. What particularly riled him was the attack on his *morals*. He could never tolerate the least insinuation that his integrity was not beyond reproach. Indeed, so strong were his feelings that his gratitude to those friends who backed him was lifelong, and some have even attributed his strong and influential endorsement to President Roosevelt of Oliver Wendell Homes, Jr., for the Supreme Court to this factor.

Lodge's personality presented certain difficulties for a politician; he had a sharp tongue, a quick temper, a rather aristocratic air, and what at least by some might have been seen as a disdain for those less endowed with brains or breeding. But his shrewd realism, his tireless industry, his quick grasp of legislative problems, his orderly and cogent speeches, and the continued loyalty of the "shoemakers of Lynn" in his home district made him one of the major powers of the party.

His intimate friendship and constant close association with President Roosevelt was also a part of his political strength. The great Theodore depended on him for many

kinds of intellectual stimulation. Witness this letter from
the White House to Nannie Lodge, Cabot's brilliant and
charming wife:

> Would you and Cabot be willing to dine here entirely
> alone on Monday, Wednesday, Thursday or Friday? I feel
> as though I should bust if I am not to discuss at length
> and without my usual cautious reserve several ques-
> tions—Dewey, Schley, Hanna, Foraker, Cuba, Bagehot's
> Shakespeare, the Hallstadt culture as connected with
> Homer's Achaeans, the latest phase of the applied Mon-
> roe Doctrine and the Boston Mayoralty election.

Lodge had met and mildly approved of Wilson as president of Princeton, but he does not seem really to have fo-
cused on him until 1912, when it came to his attention that
the governor of New Jersey had substantially changed his
political creed from right to left. Lodge was certainly an
economic conservative, but he was by no means a dyed-in-
the-wool exponent of laissez-faire. The seas and winds of
the old clipper-ship era seemed for him to have cleansed his
dollars to a brighter hue than the oil and rails of the new
and vulgar tycoons, and he had little sympathy with the ar-
rogance and crude manners of some of these self-made
men. Not, however, that he didn't know how to make use
of them! But what he objected to in Wilson was not so
much his new doctrine as the speed with which he had
abandoned the old. In a letter he expressed this opinion:

> As to Wilson, I think he is a man of ability, but he has no
> intellectual integrity at all. A man can change one or

two of his opinions for his own advantage and change them perfectly honestly, but when a man changes all the well-considered opinions of a lifetime and changes them all at once for his own popular advantage, it seems to me that he must lack in loyalty of conviction. . . . I think he would sacrifice any opinion at any moment for his own benefit and go back to it the next moment if he thought returning to it would be profitable.

It did not add to Lodge's opinion of Wilson that Roosevelt's defection from the Republican Party in the Chicago convention of 1912, probably the most agonizing event of Lodge's political life, handed the election to the Democrats. It might not be true to say that he disliked Democrats, but he certainly regarded them as occupying a lower level of creation than his own party. And the bitterness of seeing his closest friend and hero become a mugwump after what they had both gone through in 1884 could only increase the natural acidity of his temper. He preserved his precious friendship with the Bull Moose candidate—nothing on earth would have induced him to forgo that—and he spoke no word against him in the campaign, but he stumped and voted for Taft. His party loyalty would always be his first rule.

As there were two Wilsons, so were there two Lodges, and it was certainly a great pity that every confrontation between the two men brought out the lesser man in each. Mrs. Winthrop Chanler, a member of the intimate circle of the Roosevelts and Lodges, emphasized Lodge's dual nature in her memoir *Roman Spring* and attributed to the animosity of Boston's Back Bay in the Blaine campaign the accentuation of "a certain ready-to-fight element in Cabot's character." She added that in discussions he was one of those who care more for downing their adversary than for discovering common ground for possible agreement. While admitting that she was not painting an agreeable picture of her friend, she nonetheless insisted that "under the captious crustiness there was a very real man whom one could not but like, respect and grow to love." And she ended on this note:

> His fine library was an essential part of him and he was at his best when, at the end of an evening—there might have been a dinner party at his house and all but two or three of the guests departed,—he would take down one volume and then another, reading some line of prose or verse with an intimate sense of their meaning and beauty. He then thawed into a most sympathetic and "belovable" person, representing no longer the harshness of Plymouth Rock, but the pleasant laureled dingles of Parnassus. He knew and loved books with most intelligent affection.

Wilson's successful attempt, early in his first term, to have Congress lift the exemption for American coastwise shipping from tolls in the Panama Canal, correcting an injustice to other nations stemming from the Hay-Pauncefote Treaties, met with Lodge's enthusiastic approval, but it was to be one of the last subjects on which the two agreed. The outbreak of war in Europe was to divide them irrevocably.

Lodge, like Roosevelt, started out as a technical neutral.

He sided with the majority of his fellow citizens in not wishing the nation to become involved—at least in the fighting. And in the old Yankee tradition he was still suspicious of the imperial ambitions of Great Britain and jealous of her rule of the seas. But when the conflict in Europe began to take on the aspect of the struggle of freedom-loving peoples against the mailed fist of Teutonic absolutism, when the threat to the very existence of England and France began to loom and the horrid prospect of America standing alone against a world-conquering Germany became an actual possibility, Lodge and Roosevelt both turned vociferous in their support of the Allied cause.

It obliterated all trace of Lodge's old prejudice against Britain. After all, it was the land of his heritage, the home of his favorite poets and writers, the residence of many of his friends. Had he not been a constant visitor to its shores? And had he not lovingly toured the great cathedrals of France with his friend Adams? What had the strutting Prussian Junkers to offer a sober-minded Brahmin from Boston?

A first clash with Wilson arose over the latter's support of a bill to authorize the federal government to purchase the vessels of German registry moored for the duration in American ports. The argument for the bill was that they were needed to supplement our inadequate merchant marine and that they would be immune from Allied sinking (should the Allies decline to recognize the change in registry) by being used in a distant South American trade, where they could release American vessels for needed service in the Atlantic. The arguments against it were that the money paid for the ships would aid the German war effort and that the bill was a socialist intrusion by government into the shipping business.

Lodge led the opposition that defeated the bill with a venom and animosity which aroused equal feeling in the president, who exclaimed: "The influences that have so long dominated legislation and administration here are making their last and most desperate stand to regain their control." He threatened the opposing congressmen with no quarter: "We must hit them and hit them straight in the face and not mind if the blood comes."

Lodge was even more violent. He professed to believe that Wilson was actually pro-German, that, like many college professors, his ideas were based "on German thought, German books and German writers." He even went so far as to insinuate that the president's son-in-law, McAdoo, who was sponsoring the bill, was allied in some sinister fashion with the German partners of Kuhn Loeb! He accused Wilson of cowardice, asserting that he flinched in the presence of danger, both physical and moral. And he wrote to Roosevelt: "I never expected to hate anyone in politics with the hatred I feel towards Wilson."

John A. Garraty in his life of Lodge had the courtesy to allow his subject's grandson and namesake to supply this gloss on the last quotation: "If by the word 'hatred' is meant the usual dictionary definition of an emotion which is not only malevolent, malignant and malicious, but also continuing, steady and permanent, then there was no hatred between the two men. That there was political hatred for limited periods of time, is the most that can in justice be said."

This is reminiscent of President Clinton's quibbling definition of embarrassing terms at his impeachment hearings. I find the dictionary definition exact in expressing what Lodge felt toward Wilson.

Another factor that added to Lodge's low opinion of the president was the latter's remarriage to Mrs. Galt only fifteen months after the death of his first wife. Lodge had suffered the sad loss of his own lovely spouse, to whom he had been so happily wed for forty-four years, just two months before, and his private remarks about Wilson's quick recovery from a much demonstrated grief were not complimentary.

When Wilson addressed Congress with his eloquent call for a declaration of war against Germany, Lodge relented so far as to take his hand as he was leaving the Capitol and tell him: "Mr. President, you have expressed in the loftiest manner possible the sentiments of the American people." And he wrote to Mrs. Brooks Adams: "For the first time he spoke as a President ought to, and all his recommendations were good."

But the lull in their feud was brief. Lodge waxed indignant at the wartime powers that Wilson necessarily assumed and angrily derided what he deemed his misuse of them. His intemperate language in private gatherings eventually brought down on him the deliberate reproach of his old friend Henry Adams.

This is how Ernest Samuels related the scene in his life of Adams:

One day at Adams's table in the presence of Spring-Rice and his wife, Lodge launched out on a particularly violent denunciation of his adversary in the White House. As the story has it, Adams finally struck the board with his whitened and trembling fist. "Cabot, I've never allowed treasonable conversation at this table, and I don't propose to allow it now." The two men were, of course, soon reconciled, but it was clear that Adams felt that the time of irresponsible partisanship had passed.

9

WHEN WILSON RETURNED to Washington in the summer of 1919 at the conclusion of his second and final stay in Paris, with the proposed Treaty of Versailles in his pocket, his first efforts to win the approval of the Senate were conciliatory. He invited key members of that body to dinner at the White House, urging them to make no public assessments of the treaty until he had had the chance to explain his views to them. Senator Lodge was even asked to take Edith Wilson in to dinner.

But the president had spoiled it all in Lodge's view by having, prior to the dinner, gone up to Boston to express those views in public. "Mr. Wilson has asked me to dinner," he sniffed. "He also asked me to say nothing. He then goes to my own town and makes a speech—very characteristic."

Lodge had little to say at the White House gathering. He asked three questions and told people afterward that he had learned nothing.

The forces for and against the ratification of the treaty were at first more or less evenly matched. Despite the deep opposition in the Republican Senate majority to Article 10 of the Covenant of the League, which mandated that the United States, even unwillingly, should take a military part in any action that the member nations should decree against an aggressor, there was widespread public approval of some sort of world peace organization and an almost universal yearning for a quick treaty to end the still technically unended war. Enthusiasts for the latter found it hard to understand why the treaty and the league couldn't be taken up separately, and peace declared, so to speak, overnight, but the administration insisted that the two had been joined as a unit by the nations in Paris and couldn't be reconsidered individually here. The result was that Article 10 predominated over the minor and controversial boundary revisions contained in the treaty, and the real dispute centered on it.

When Wilson was warned by the Democratic leader in the Senate that a two-thirds majority might not be obtainable to ratify the treaty as it stood, he exclaimed: "Anyone who opposes me in that, I'll crush!" This, in view of the fact that his was now a minority party, seems almost megalomaniacal. But Wilson was probably already aware that he was facing the greatest battle of his lifetime, when everything that he had dreamed that it might be his destiny to accomplish was at stake, and he was accordingly tense.

It was equally Lodge's greatest battle, a struggle for his truculent but passionate belief in an America geographically and morally isolated from what he saw as a world of imperialistic exploiters, an America wrapped in the shining armor of the Monroe Doctrine and supported by such warriors as his recently departed hero, the great Theodore. Might not the sweep of Article 10 even prevent America from imposing the restrictions on immigration that Lodge approved? And who could have much faith in a peace organization made up of nations that had drafted so vindictive and unjust a treaty?

Lodge saw that time might be on his side as the full effect of the Article 10 commitment sank into the public consciousness. He consumed two full weeks in reading the entire text of the treaty aloud to the empty chamber of the Foreign Affairs Committee. His grandson offered this excuse for such a delaying tactic in another note to Garraty's biography: "Reading aloud the entire text of a treaty or other document is not an unusual device in the Senate. . . . It is not such a heinous crime to ask people to know the actual facts about the subject they are so vehemently discussing." But Lodge *knew* that no one was listening!

With the beginning of the hearings countless witnesses, some of dubious importance, some of strong animus against the administration, were called. Secretary of State Lansing, who had once said of his chief that "entrenched within the White House, he was impregnable in his self-righteousness and imprisoned within his own certainties," did Wilson's cause no good when he testified that, ignored in Paris, he had had little to do with the drafting of the treaty. And Lodge saw to it that demands were constantly made to the administration for documents, some of which were indignantly refused.

Did Lodge count on Wilson's hurting his own crusade by shows of bad temper brought on by the committee's tactics? It's hard to say, but when a friend asked him if

Wilson's personal hostility wasn't a slender thread on which to hang our "salvation from the League," he retorted: "It's as strong as a cable with its strands wired and twisted together!"

Wilson as a committee witness attempted to soften the fears of those who apprehended that America could be forced into a war of which she disapproved, with the subtle but specious argument that her obligation to act was moral rather than legal and thus subject to the judgment of Congress. He said this in reply to a question by Senator Warren G. Harding, his successor-to-be in the White House:

> When I speak of a legal obligation I mean one that specifically binds you to do a particular thing under certain sanctions. . . . Now a moral obligation is of course superior to a legal obligation, and, if I may say so, has a greater binding force, only there always remains in the moral obligation the right to exercise one's judgment as to whether it is indeed incumbent upon one in those circumstances to do that thing. In every moral obligation there is an element of judgment. In a legal obligation there is no element of judgment.

This was not Wilson at his best; this was the Wilson that many of his political opponents distrusted. Under cross-questioning he finally admitted that America's duty under the covenant would be a "legal obligation with a moral sanction."

Lodge for a time refused to present any amendments to the treaty, taking the position that such were the business of the executive branch, and that, besides, any amendment to the document would require its laborious resubmission to the nations already signatory. But when Elihu Root, an ever resourceful lawyer, came up with the suggestion that a "reservation" as opposed to an amendment would not require such resubmission, Lodge, with the aid of one other senator, Porter J. McCumber, redrafted Article 10 to read: "The United States assumes no obligation to preserve the territorial integrity or political independence of any country or to interfere in controversies between nations . . . under the provisions of Article 10 . . . unless in any particular case the Congress, which, under the Constitution, has the sole power to declare war or authorize the employment of the military or naval forces of the United States, shall by act or joint resolution so provide."

Wilson rejected the reservation out of hand. He claimed that it not only would require resubmission of the treaty but would wreck the whole concept of world government. In September he made his fateful decision to tour the nation in a desperate effort to persuade the people in a series of public addresses to make it known to their elected representatives that they backed their president in his program for a better and saner world.

The trip was planned by Tumulty. It would last for just under a month and take the president to the West Coast, passing through the western and midwestern states, where isolationist sentiment was strongest. The South was too firmly Democratic to need persuasion, and the Northeast was too Republican to be wooed. With the president on board his private car, the *Mayflower*, was Dr. Grayson, who always went with him; his stenographer, Swem; and, of course, Edith Wilson, to be sure that her beloved husband was well cared for and didn't overdo. The exhausting schedule called for thirty major speeches, and it would all end, as we have seen, with Wilson's collapse in Wichita. His continually failing health, however, did not keep him from moments of soaring eloquence. Hear him in St. Louis:

> You are betrayed. You fought for something that you did not get. And the glory of the armies and the navies of the United States is gone like a dream in the night, and there ensues upon it, in the suitable darkness of the night, the nightmare of dread which lay upon the nations before this war came; and there will come some time, in the vengeful Providence of God, another war in which not a few hundred thousand men from America will have to die, but as many millions as are necessary to accomplish the final freedom of the peoples of the world.

On his return to Washington he remained essentially invisible for weeks, but in time a weak and petulant invalid appeared in a wheelchair. If he was taken for a drive, he not only insisted that his chauffeur not exceed a speed of twenty miles an hour, but sent the Secret Service men to arrest any driver who passed them. Of course, these men would pretend to make a chase and then return to say that the culprit had got away. And his oddities were not, unfortunately, confined to such trivia. He actually demanded and received Lansing's resignation as secretary of state when he learned that the latter had called for and presided over cabinet meetings during his illness! Worse still, he appointed in his place a little-known New York lawyer, Bainbridge Colby, whom House regarded as totally unfit for the post.

Eventually legislators began to wonder if Wilson was competent to remain in office, and an interview with the president was requested of Tumulty by Senator Albert B. Fall of New Mexico, a Republican hostile to Wilson personally, and Senator Gilbert M. Hitchcock of Nebraska, the Democratic minority leader, who was friendly to him. The real purpose of the visit was to be concealed in the pretext of a discussion of what action should be taken in the case of William O. Jenkins, an American consular agent in Puebla, Mexico, who had been kidnapped and was being held by Carranza's militia.

The interview, carefully staged by Edith, was in the president's dimly lit bedroom, where he lay on his bed, propped up by pillows, his left arm covered with a blanket. The tension in the beginning was relaxed by Grayson's suddenly hurrying into the room with the news, just received, that Jenkins had been released. Wilson's articulation was thick but understandable, and both senators agreed that he made perfect sense. But what kind of test was it of a man's presidential abilities to subject him to a few minutes' conversation with two congressmen, one a staunch member of his party? Leaving, Fall told Wilson: "We've been praying for you, sir," to which the president retorted: "Which way, Senator?"

Pressure was now exerted on Wilson from his own party, his friends, and his advisers to accept the treaty with the Lodge reservations. Colonel House and Henry White sent word that they were in favor of it, and the British and French indicated that they would have no objection. The great thing was to get a treaty signed and America into a league of nations even if she wouldn't commit herself to fight in a war that, after all, might never come. But Wilson was adamant. He insisted that he hadn't the moral right to go back on what he had signed in France.

Even Edith was at last persuaded to add her voice to the others. She may well have feared that the constant pressure on her husband was causing him more physical damage than would even the painful changing of his position on the league. Senator Hitchcock described how she told him to wait at the door of the president's bedroom while she went in and implored her husband: "For my sake, won't you accept these reservations and get this awful thing settled?" But Wilson simply took her hand in his and remonstrated: "Little girl, don't you desert me. That I cannot stand."

On November 19, 1919, the Senate voted, 55 to 39, not to ratify the treaty without the reservations. Thereafter, due to strong pressure from the administration, it voted not to ratify the treaty *with* the reservations. Wilson would rather have nothing than a treaty mutilated, as he saw it, by Lodge.

On hearing the news from the Senate, the president reached for a Bible and had this verse from Saint Paul's Epistle to the Corinthians read to him: "We are troubled on every side but not distressed. We are perplexed but not in despair." Then he commented: "If I were not a Christian, I think I should go mad, but my faith in God holds me to the belief that He is in some way working out His own plans."

Lodge's reaction was predictably different. When Elihu Root wrote to congratulate him for his handling of the non-ratification, which he labeled "one of the greatest examples of parliamentary leadership that I have ever known," Lodge replied:

"If Wilson had not written his letter to the Democratic caucus, calling on them to kill the treaty rather than accept the reservations, the treaty would have been ratified on the 19th of November. There would have been enough Democrats voting with us to have done it. It was killed by Wilson. He has been the marplot from the beginning. All the delays and all the troubles have been made by him. . . . We have worked for more than two months over those reservations and they represent an amount of labor and modification and concession that it would take me a long time to explain to you. He can have the treaty ratified at any moment if he accepts the reservations and if he declines to do so we are not in the least afraid to meet him at the polls on that issue."

Posterity, however, has tended to side more with Wilson than with Lodge. But to ex-president Taft it was a question of a plague on both their houses. Lodge and Wilson, he wrote, "exalt their personal prestige and the saving of their ugly faces above the welfare of the country and the world."

Wilson has received plaudits from many historians for his lofty concept of world peace. But it has always seemed to me that it is a simple matter for a man to dream of peace and leagues and international understandings. The whole trick in such matters is not to dream them but to implement those dreams. Wilson wouldn't accept second best, but wasn't second best a good deal better than nothing? America once in the league might have been perfectly willing to supply armed force to any army that her fellow members sought to send against an aggressor. Indeed, the very fact that she could not have been compelled to do so might have rendered her more willing. In our day we have seen a president enthusiastically undertake an unallied bombing of Iraq even when some of our fellow nations showed a marked disapproval.

That second Woodrow Wilson of whom we have spoken, crippled with a stroke, may have acted in the treaty fight as the earlier and healthier one never would have. Is it possible that the blame for our failure to enter the league may be attributable more to Edith Wilson and Cary Grayson, who hid the condition of their husband and patient from the cabinet and Congress and persuaded him to retain an office for which he was unfit, than to the isolationism of Henry Cabot Lodge?

10

THE REST OF Wilson's second term was a dreary time for him. He was a ghost of his former self and the ghost of a president. Edith in her memoirs says that Dr. Francis X. Dercum gave her this advice: "Madame, it is a grave situation, but I think you can solve it. Have everything come to you; weigh the importance of each matter and see if it is possible by consultations . . . to solve it without the guidance of your husband. . . . Always bear in mind that every time you take him a new anxiety or problem you are turning a knife in an open wound." It seems to me most unlikely that a doctor would have taken it on himself to give such drastic advice where the governance of the nation was at stake; at any rate he was conveniently dead when Edith saw fit to make public his alleged recommendation. It is certain, anyway, that the program so outlined was what Edith followed.

When Grayson, however, in a moment of sanity, had warned the Democratic leaders going to the San Francisco convention in 1920 of the impossibility of running Wilson as a third-term candidate, and James M. Cox, the governor of Ohio, had been nominated, Wilson had to face the fact that his political career was over. He had a poor opinion of

Cox, which was not improved when the new candidate ousted Wilson's friend Homer Cummings from the chairmanship of the Democratic National Committee. "It is a terrible mistake," he complained. "If Governor Cox . . . continues that course . . . his administration will be a failure, and will end in a guffaw." He added: "You know, I would rather be hated than be the object of derision."

He might have been thinking of the bitter adage of Finlay Peter Dunne: "Americans should build their triumphal arches out of bricks that could be pulled loose and flung at the hero."

Wilson had nothing, however, but enthusiasm for the vice-presidential candidate, who had been his able assistant secretary of the navy, and when, after the lost election, in the summer of 1921, Franklin Roosevelt was stricken with polio, many messages were exchanged between the two, the ailing ex-president writing letters of encouragement to the slowly recovering patient who would succeed him in the White House in twelve years' time.

Wilson met the end of his term of office with coolness and dignity. At the final meeting of his cabinet he simply said: "Gentlemen, it is one of the handicaps of my physical condition that I cannot control myself as I have been accustomed to do. God bless you all," and shook the hand of each. At the Capitol Senator Lodge announced to him that the Sixty-eighth Congress was ready to adjourn, to which he replied, after a momentary glare at his old opponent: "Tell them I have no further communications to make."

Leaving the White House, Wilson moved to a handsome

brick-and-limestone residence in S Street, purchased by a group of admiring friends—for the Wilsons had little capital of their own—where he would quietly pass the last three years of his life, watched over by the careful, the much too careful Edith. She continued to be jealous of anyone else who might share her intimacy with her husband. Colonel House, back in New York, was never allowed to visit, even for the briefest call, and now she directed her sights against Joe Tumulty, the devoted secretary who had practically merged his life with that of the president for eight years. Poor Joe, whom the proud Edith, of old southern planters' blood, considered a cheap political hack, at last gave her her chance, and she seized it.

Cox, the unsuccessful Democratic nominee, was to be the guest of honor at the Jefferson Day dinner at the National Democratic Club in New York, and Tumulty had tried unsuccessfully to obtain from Wilson a friendly message to be read there. He made the mistake, however, of supposing that his talk with Wilson justified him in writing a statement of what he took to be the ex-president's greeting, and this was delivered at the dinner. Alas, it was widely construed to be Wilson's endorsement of Cox for the presidential nomination in 1924, and Wilson refused ever to see Tumulty again.

Bainbridge Colby, Wilson's last secretary of state, talked his former chief into forming the partnership of Wilson and Colby for the practice of law, and a spacious office was taken in Washington. But the idea was ludicrous from the start. Wilson was in no state to accomplish any kind of serious work, and his extreme conscientiousness inhibited him from accepting any business that presented the least conflict of interest or that seemed inconsistent with his position as a former chief of state. The firm was soon dissolved.

Toward the end of 1923 it was evident that Wilson was rapidly failing. He liked to quote John Quincy Adams's answer to inquiries about his health: "Mr. Adams is all right, but the house he lives in is dilapidated, and it looks as if he would have to move out." The end came on February 3, 1924.

The Senate appointed a delegation to attend the funeral, and Lodge was selected to be one of that delegation. Edith sent him a handwritten note: "Realizing that your presence would be embarrassing to you and unwelcome to me, I write to request that you do not attend."

Lodge replied: "You may rest assured that nothing would be more distasteful to me than to do anything which by any possibility could be unwelcome to you."

Colonel House wrote the following to Charles Seymour, the editor of his *Intimate Papers*, four year later:

> There were many doors to the temples that men of old reared to their gods, to the sun, to the moon, to the mythical deities, Isis, Jupiter, Mars. Behind the innermost door dwelt the mysteries. And now you who have had access to my most intimate papers ask me to unlock the innermost door, a door to which I have no key. My separation from Woodrow Wilson was and is to me a tragic mystery, a mystery that now can never be dis-

pelled, for its explanation lies buried with him. Theories I have, and theories they must remain.

Never during the years we worked together, was there an unkind or impatient word, written or spoken, and this to me is an abiding consolation.

While our friendship was not of long duration it was as close as human friendships grow to be. To this his letters and mine bear silent testimony. Until a shadow fell between us I never had a more considerate friend, and my devotion to his memory remains and will remain unchanged.

But the key that must unlock the innermost door may still be found. It may be discovered in the last word that Woodrow Wilson uttered: "Edith."

Select Bibliography

Any reader wishing to study Wilson in depth must consult these two massive studies:

Baker, Roy Stannard. *Woodrow Wilson, Life and Letters.* 8 vols.: *Youth, Princeton, Governor, President, Neutrality, Facing War, War Leader, Armistice.* Garden City, N.Y.: Doubleday, 1927–39.

Link, Arthur Stanley. *Wilson.* 5 vols.: *The Road to the White House, The New Freedom, The Struggle for Neutrality, Confusions and Crises, Campaigns for Progressivism and Peace.* Princeton, N.J.: Princeton University Press, 1947–65.

The following is a perhaps adequate sample of Wilson's own numerous works:

Congressional Government. Boston: Houghton Mifflin, 1885.

Constitutional Government in the United States. New York: Columbia University Press, 1908.

Division and Reunion. New York: Longmans Green, 1909.

George Washington. New York: Harper & Bros., 1897.

A History of the American People. New York: Harper & Bros., 1902.

Books on Wilson are innumerable. All I can say is that I have found the following illuminating:

Brogden, Henry W. *Woodrow Wilson, the Academic Years.*

Cambridge, Mass.: Belknap Press, Harvard University Press, 1967.

Cooper, John Milton, Jr. *The Warrior and the Priest: Woodrow Wilson and Theodore Roosevelt*. Cambridge, Mass., 1983.

Garraty, John A. *Henry Cabot Lodge*. New York, 1953.

———. *Woodrow Wilson*. New York: Knopf, 1956.

George, Alexander, and Juliet George. *Woodrow Wilson and Colonel House*. New York: J. Day & Co., 1956.

Grayson, Cary. *Woodrow Wilson, an Intimate Study*. New York: Holt, Rinehart & Winston, 1960.

Heckscher, August. *Woodrow Wilson*. Charles Scribner's Sons, 1991.

McAdoo, Eleanor Wilson, ed. *The Priceless Gift: The Love Letters of Woodrow Wilson and Ellen Axson*. New York: McGraw-Hill, 1962.

Nevins, Allen. *Henry White*. New York, 1930.

Seymour, Charles, ed. *The Intimate Papers of Colonel House*. Boston: Houghton Mifflin, 1926–28.

Smith, Gene. *When the Cheering Stopped*. New York: Morrow, 1964.

Steel, Ronald. *Walter Lippmann*. Boston: Little, Brown, 1980.

Tribble, Edwin, ed. *A President in Love: The Courtship Letters of Woodrow Wilson and Edith Bolling Galt*. Boston: Houghton Mifflin, 1981.

Tumulty, Joseph. *Woodrow Wilson as I Knew Him*. Garden City, N.Y.: Doubleday, 1920.

Viereck, George. *The Strangest Friendship in History*. New York: Liveright, 1937.

Weinstein, Edwin A. *Woodrow Wilson, a Medical and Psychological Biography*. Princeton, N.J.: Princeton University Press, 1981.

Wilson, Edith Bolling. *My Memoir*. Indianapolis, 1918.